Loretta Santini

75

CITIES OF ITALY

Publication authorised by

Consorzio per la Tutela del Palio di Siena

SIENA

GUIDE WITH TOWN PLAN

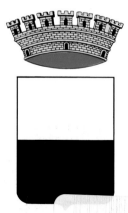

Dis
**FABIC
Via B. Tolomei,
SIENA

D1051845

CENTRO STAMPA EDITORIALE

plurigraf

PERSEUS

PG-SII-01

SIENA

An overall picture

To the tourist arriving here either by the ancient road of Francigena or Romea, or else via the modern-day route from Florence, Siena appears in a gradual shading of brick-red buildings with their roof-tiles in ascending layers, the city branches and spreads out over the hills, with elongated houses, slim church steeples that sudden-ly go uphill and downdale; all in a lively and uneven landscape that is dominated by the contours of the monumental buildings.

Situated on the heights and prac-tically in the centre of southern Tuscany, the city of Siena rises up on the ridge of three hills that ex-tend from Croce del travaglio, the topographic centre of the built up area. Also branching out from here are the three ridgeways which go to make up the city's road net-work, namely Via di Città, Banchi di Sopra and Banchi di Sotto. These roads continue along the ridge leading into other roads un-til they arrive at the most impor-tant gates (or Porte) of the last of the city walls to be constructed and which still stand to this very day.

They are Porta San Marco which leads to Grosseto, Porta Camollia which leads to Florence and Porta Romana which, as the name sug-gests, leads to Rome. The actual nucleus of the city is, therefore, modelled according to the lay out of these three hills that are sepa-rated by as many steep and al-most impregnable valleys, large parts of which are today still in their natural state or else cultivat-ed into gardens and orchards. It follows that from the very begin-ning the city's perimeter assumed a winding and characteristic ap-

pearance roughly in the shape of a star and which remained un-changed in spite of the city's fur-ther development. The clayey na-ture of the soil is linked to another of the city's characteristics, that is the presence of a number of springs which, in the past, greatly influenced Siena's actual exis-tence: hence the need to strength-en them. The Sienese, in fact, right from very ancient times, tried their hardest to exploit even the small-est trickle from the subterranean layer of clay, channelling the water into the numerous public foun-

tains and private wells, via a long network of criss-crossing underground tunnels. Among the public fountains, the most famous ones are Fonte di Follonica, Fonte d'Ovile, Fonte Nuova, Fonte Gaia and, most of all, Fonte Branda, the oldest and most abundant in water, situated at the foot of a cliff.

At the edge of this cliff stands the church of St. Dominic which in the past aided the development of industries and contributed towards making the inhabitants of the neighbourhood wealthy. At first glance, the whole of Siena seems to be enclosed within the mighty circle of its medieval walls, clinging to its hills, with its buildings terraced on the slopes. Very few towns present such sharp differences in their ground levels and offer such varied and interesting panoramic views. From the windows of the houses, the steep streets and the roads skirting the edges of the valleys, the view dominates the surrounding undulating countryside and sweeps the distant horizon, especially to the South and Southeast, where the landscape is wide and spacious.

Right up to Mount Amiata and the heights in front of the lakes of Chiusi, Montepulciano and Valdichiana.

On entering the city, one notices straightaway that the roads paved with cobblestones are without pavements. The buildings are tall and lined one up against another, often not allowing even the side roads to separate them. In fact, when passing underneath the houses, one will find arches linking parallel roads, some suggestive courtyards and dark, closed-in entrance halls, intricate lanes and narrow, small squares. All these aspects give Siena its very fascinating appearance and, together, form its history without which nobody could ever understand this very characteristic city, this corner of the Middle Ages that has succeeded in reaching us, which does not exist exclusively for its splendid monuments and for its numerous works of art, save that alongside this miracle of art stands the city itself: a city of distant even though uncertain and legendary origins.

Historical Outline

The origins of Siena are lost in legend. One tradition has it that its name is derived from the Gallic tribe of the Senones, another that it is of Roman origin. It was certainly a Roman colony (Sena Iulia), and to this day one can see, at the corners of its streets and squares, the Roman she-wolf with the twins, testifying to the fact that it belonged to the imperial city.

It was, however, in the Middle Ages that Siena reached the height of its importance and it is precisely this period which has left the most significant marks upon it: the walls, the gates, the narrow, winding alley-ways, and the houses huddled together irregu-

larly are still those that stood there in the long feudal period.

After having been ruled first by the Longobards and then by the Franks, it passed, towards the middle of the 11th century, into the hands of the Prince-Bishops. Half-way through the 12th century, these in turn were overthrown by the Consuls who set up a secular government to replace that of the clergy. It was in this period that Siena attained its greatest political importance and territorial expansion, due mostly to economic factors.

Indeed, it was economic rather than political reasons which shortly afterwards led to its rivalry with the other large and prosperous city of Tuscany; the Florence of the Guelphs. By supporting the Ghibelline faction and harbouring the Florentine exiles, Siena set itself up as an open rival.

This struggle came to a head in 1260 when, at Monteaperti, the people of Siena, under the command of Provenzano Salvani and Farinata degli Uberti, defeated the Florentines in a terrific and bloody battle.

Siena was now at the height of its fortunes and, after the fall of the Consuls, power was conferred upon a Podestà, supported by the Captain of the People (1252).

However, after the Battle of Monteaperti, there began the slow decline of its prosperity and power. The Pope's excommunication of the Ghibelline city, together with other economic and political factors, soon induced the wealthy Sienese merchants to go over to the Guelph faction, the more readily to ensure the profits of their trade. At the same time, King Manford died, the ally who had supported the Ghibellines at the Battle of Monteaperti.

In 1269, all this led to the reaction of the Guelphs in Tuscany, under leadership of Florence, which brought about the final defeat of Siena, and when the Ghibelline faction had thus been overthrown, the city itself also went over to the Guelphs.

Under the Council of Nine, which was established in 1287 and remained in power until 1355, Siena was still at the height of its splendour: it was at this time that the Town Hall, the new Cathedral and other important private and public buildings were erected, bearing eloquent witness to the Gothic style which had already been asserting itself for some time.

However, the city's liberty and political and economic power gradually declined. Between 1399 and 1404, the city was governed by first the Visconti and then the Petrucci. This was followed by Spanish rule from 1531 to 1552: torn by internal strife, and external disputes between one feudal lord and another, and consequently, between one State and another, Siena was now completely at the mercy of the larger powers.

The occupation of the city on the orders of Charles V, King of Spain, under the pretext of garrisoning it in order to put an end to the continual fighting, caused a violent rebellion in 1552. However, European politics were too intricate and too much concerned with conflicting interests, and Siena's internal situation was by now too weak, for it to be able to maintain its independence. Thus, in 1559, it was once again subjected to foreign rule, this time to that of the Medici, who were allies of Spain.

It remained under the rule of the Duchy of Tuscany until the formation of the Kingdom of Italy. From that time on, its history has been bound up with that of the latter.

Artistic outline

Art was for Siena a true mirror of an extremely compound and variegated society, but exceptionally up-to-date in its tastes and customs even in the poor classes; a society whose groups and members right from the State Bench to the Guilds of craftsmen, from the

5

great monastic communities to the popular brotherhoods, all consider art as an indispensable attribute to their dignity, or rather, their actual existence. And even if the beginnings of such a dazzling and prolonged art tradition were modest and tardy in coming, in the space of a few centuries Siena acquired its rich, artistic patrimony, for which it is so rightly renowned. The 12th century saw the construction of many beautiful buildings, numerous towers and nobles' residences, churches of modest dimensions though pure romanesque in their architecture, namely San Pietro alla Magione, San Donato, San Cristofaro, San Marco and San Quirico. Others unfortunately have either been destoyed or incorporated in successive constructions. The buildings changed all of a sudden from these minor works to the truly great national enterprise of the Cathedral, which summarises in the complex story of its construction, the Sienese architectural leanings from the fall of Romanesque to the birth of Gothic. The flourishing Gothic architecture can be witnessed in many splendid Sienese buildings, take for example the upper part of the Cathedral's facade, the apse which was much later enlarged, and the vaults above the main nave.

The Gothic period saw the construction of the Baptistry facade and the huge churches of the Mendicant Orders, such as St. Francis, St. Dominic and St. Mary of the Servants, wherein the spacious interiors seem to diminish and vanish in the shadows of the tall exposed beams and fit in with the vast expanses of the side walls with their high ogival windows. In the two centuries during which the Cathedral was built, Siena acquired its most characteristic features and developed its own unmistakable style even in civil ar-

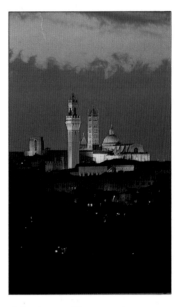

chitecture. The most accomplished work and highest expression of this style is Palazzo Pubblico, which later inspired the design of the other city buildings such as Palazzo Sansedoni, Chigi-Saraceni, Palazzo del Capitano and even Palazzo Marsili and Palazzo Buonsignori that were constructed in the mid-15th century.

Originating from this style and representing a typical motif of the local architecture is the «*Sienese arch*», which is a combination of two elements of Pisan origin, the barrier-type arch and the Muslim-type deep sickle arch. Sienese architecture displays its originality even in the fountains and gates: the aforementioned Fonte d'Ovile, Fonte di Follonica and the famous Fontebranda, as well as Porta Romana, Porta Pispini and Porta d'Ovile, which were built not only for defence purposes, but also to give a grand stateliness to the main gateways to the city. In the early 15th century, Siena too welcomed the novelties of the Renaissance period, with the works of the two Florentines,

Bernardo Rossellini and Giuliano da Maiano, and the Sienese Antonio Federighi (1420-1490), Francesco di Giorgio Martini (1439-1502) and Baldassare Peruzzi (1481-1536).

During the Baroque period, the architects working in Siena were Damiano Schifandini, Flaminio del Turco, Giovanni Fontana and Benedetto Giovanelli, who are all attributed with numerous buildings of a harmonious and well-proportioned style.

In the field of sculpture, Siena did not have any particular school until the arrival of Nicola and Giovanni Pisano, the former sculptured the magnificent pulpit of the Cathedral and the latter the statues of the facade, and they both had numerous and very valid followers.

Sienese sculpture later reached supreme heights with Jacopo della Quercia whose creations include Fonte Gaia and certain parts of Fonte Battesimale, which incidentally Ghiberti and Donatello also worked on. Siena reached the highest acclaims in art mainly with its paintings. After Guido da Siena's *Madonna*, one of the first great Sienese paintings, comes Duccio di Buoninsegna, who is considered the founder of the Sienese school and who found the Gothic style ideally suited to his own spirit. Then come Simone Martini and the Lorenzetti's who bequeathed Siena their greatest works and who also had a faithful band of followers amongst whom stand out for their personality and style, Barna, Taddeo di Bartolo, Jacopo di Mino del Pelliccciaio and Paolo di Giovanni Fei.

Also the successive centuries brought some famous names to Sienese painting, names such as Sassetta, Giovanni di Paolo, Vecchietta, Matteo di Giovanni, Francesco di Giorgio Martini in the 15th century and Sodoma, Domenico Beccafumi and Baldas-

sare Meruzzi in the 16th century.

With the coming of Mannerism, the Sienese school suffered a decline and was left without any masters of great importance. But it should be pointed out that the Sienese also achieved great perfection in the minor arts. Goldsmiths, inlayers, miniaturists, all excelled in those works where the artisan technique was combined with their elegant sense of decoration and the most authentic expression of their creative talent.

THE CITY AND THE PALIO

There are few Italian cities which, like Siena, are so complete and organic from the artistic point of view as to as to make them archetypes of a particular style and period.

Siena still preserves intact its medieval aspect: it is built on three hills; full of steep, winding alleyways, enclosed within the circle of its massive walls (some seven kilometres in length) which seem to safeguard its culture and the treasures of its art and history.

THE PALIO

For a city such as this, with its ancient aspect still intact, a festival or rather a tradition like this revives to some extent the tone and colour of the past, brought to life again in the present.

With its long tradition the Palio is today certainly one of the most popular of Italian festivals, attracting many thousands of people every year from every part of the world.

It takes place twice a year: on July 2, (to commemorate the miracles of the Madonna of Provenzano) and on August 16, (to honour the Assumption of the Virgin). The 17 «contrade» into which the city is now divided compete in it, wearing their traditional costumes and carrying their emblems. Each «contrada» has a name, a banner and a church of its own. We will give now a short list of these «contrade».

The Palio of the Districts

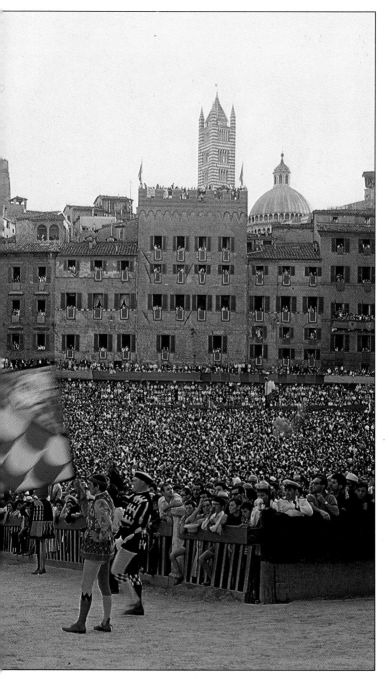

On this page:
Top: The Cathedral decked with the flags of the 17 Districts.
Left: Blessing of the horse and rider in the District Oratory on the afternoon before the race.
Following page:
Top: The "Carroccio" brings up the rear of the Historical Procession.
Bottom: The Palazzo del Comune decked with flags.

THIRD OF THE CITY

This area comprises six Districts.

The Noble Eagle District (Aquila)

Its emblem is the two-headed eagle bearing the imperial crown and against the golden sun with the letters U.I. This emblem was conceded by King Umberto in 1887, the same year in which on the 16th July both Margherita and Umberto of Savoy attended the Palio. The District's flag is yellow with blue and black stripes and the headquarters are situated in Via del Casato di Sotto.

The Snail District (Chiocciola)

The coat-of-arms bears a crawling snail in the centre set against a silvery background strewn with roses and the initials U. and M. The flag is yellow and red with a blue border. Situated in Via San Marco is the 17th century church of Saint Peter and Saint Paul, which already belonged to the suppressed convent of the Nuns of Saint Paul. Since 1814 it is the Oratory of the Snail and its offices are located in the rooms adjoining the church.

The Flag-ship of the Wave District (Capitana dell'Onda)

This District's coat-of-arms has a dolphin with the royal crown floating in a blue sea. The Wave's colours which until 1714 were white and black, now are white and pale blue. The District headquarters are in Via Giovanni Dupré, near the picturesque arch of St. Joseph. Next door to these offices is the tiny church of St. Joseph which was erected in 1522 by the Guild of Carpenters and ceded in 1787 by the Archduke Pietro Leopoldo to the Wave District.

The Panther District (Pantera)

The insignia of this District is a rampant panther set against the letter U on a red and silver shield and the District colours are red and blue with white stripes. The tiny church of St. Quirinus and St. Juliette is in Via San Quirico and since 1957 it is the Oratory of the Panther District, which has its headquarters in the same street.

The Forest District (Selva)

The coat-of-arms displays a rhinoceros under a thickly foliaged oak backed by a golden sun in a blue field with the letter U. This District flies a green and orange flag with white stripes. Looking onto the pretty square of San Sebastiano are the District's headquarters and Oratory, which passed over to them in the year 1818.

The Tortoise District (Tartuca)

The District's coat-of-arms is a tortoise in a golden field, with Savoy knots entwined with daisies. Yellow and blue are the colours of this District whose territory comprises the ancient nucleus of Siena. The Oratory was erected in 1684 by the same District residents and is dedicated to St. Anthony of Padova. Adjoining the church, in Via Tommaso Pendola, are the headquarters and museum of the Tortoise District.

THIRD OF
SAN MARTINO

This area comprises five districts.

The Prior Owl District
(Civetta)

The coat-of-arms has a crowned owl, perched on a branch against a black and red background with white details and the letters U and M. Red and black are the distinguishing colours of the Owl flag. Its headquarters are in Via Cecco Angiolieri and the adjacent medieval court of Castellare degli Ugurgieri holds the Oratory that was constructed in the year 1935 by the District residents.

The Horned Lion District
(Leocorno)

A rampant horned lion, or unicorn, stands in the centre of the coat-of-arms bordered in blue and bearing the motto «Humberti Regis Gratia». The flag is white and orange with blue stripes. The headquarters are in Via di Pantaneto near the pretty square of San Giovanni Battista in Pantaneto and are commonly called San Giovannino. Recently the Oratory was transferred here.

The Noble Conch Shell District (Nicchio)

A silver conch shell on a blue background, topped by the archducal crown, two coral sprigs and a pendant formed by the Savoy knot entwined with two Cyprus roses all go to make up the coat-of-arms of this District. The flag is blue with yellow and red stripes. The headquarters are sited in Via Pispini and nearby the District residents erected their Oratory in the year 1680.

The Vale of the Ram District (Valdimontone)

Commonly known as the Ram District for on its coat-of-arms there is a rampant ram with a crown and the letter U. The District's flag is red and yellow with white stripes. The headquarters and Oratory dedicated to St. Leonard belong to the Ram District since the year 1741 and are situated in Via di Valdimontone. Recent restoration work has returned to the pretty little church, constructed in 1173, its original romanesque aspect.

The Tower District (Torre)

The emblem of this District is an elephant bearing a tower on its back. The saddle-cloth which is red with a white cross and the small flag with a silver cross were added after the year 1877. From the 16th century the flag has always been wine red in colour with white and pale blue arabesques. Via Salicotto is the centre of the District and in this street stands the beautiful headquarters and Oratory of St. James which has belonged to the Tower District for the past four centuries.

THIRD OF CAMOLLIA

This area comprises six Districts.

The Noble Caterpillar District (Bruco)

A caterpillar creeping on a twig and wearing the archducal crown forms the emblem of this District and the coat-of-arms bears the Savoy cross. The flag is yellow and green with blue stripes. The Oratory, with the adjoining headquarters and museum, is situated in Via del Comune and was constructed in the year 1680 by the District residents and named after the «Holy Name of God».

The Dragon District (Drago)

A winged dragon, with a crown and a small flag bearing the letter U forms the coat-of-arms of this District whose colours are red and green with yellow stripes. The church of St. Catherine acts as the District's Oratory and was assigned by an archducal decree dating from 1787. The rooms adjoining the church function as the Dragon headquarters and they are located in Piazza Matteotti, which at one time was knows as «Poggio Malavolti».

The Imperial Giraffe District (Giraffa)

The coat-of-arms has a giraffe tied with a string held by a moor. A ribbon at the top bears the motto «Humbertus I dedit». The District colours are white and red. Since the year 1824, the Oratory is the lower oratory of the collegiate church of St. Mary of Provenzano, which keeps in custody the image of the Madonna of Provenzano and to which the local residents have paid homage right from the late 16th century. The headquarters are in Via delle Vergini.

The Sovereign Porcupine District (Istrice)

Its emblem is a crowned porcupine on a silver background with red Cyprus roses and the Savoy knot. The flag is white with red, black and blue arabesques. Via Camollia is the centre of the District and in this same street lies the headquarters and Oratory dedicated to St. Bartholomew. The Oratory is an ancient church of the Saints Vincent and Anastasia and it has belonged to the Porcupine District since the year 1788.

The She-Wolf District (Lupa)

The emblem is the she-wolf of Rome suckling the twins and the Sienese ensign. The white and red border has alternating red and white crosses. The flag is white and red with orange stripes. The headquarters and Oratory are situated in the 16th century church of St. Rocco in Via Vallerozzi, which already belonged to the St. Rocco Brotherhood and was then ceded to the She-Wolf District in 1786 by the Archduke.

The Noble Goose District (Oca)

A white goose with the royal crown and a blue ribbon from which hangs the Savoy cross make up the coat-of-arms of the District. The flag is white and green with red stripes. St. Catherine was born in the Fontebranda region and in her memory a Sanctuary was built on the same site where her actual house stood. The headquarters and Oratory are situated in the rooms adjoining the Sanctuary and they were constructed by the District in the year 1465.

Only 10 of these 17 «contrade» take part in the actual Palio race, through a rotation system linked to the lottery which takes place before the festival.

The actual festival begins in the afternoon, with the traditional, extremely picturesque procession. It consists of a parade, in historical costume, of mace-bearers, trumpeters, bandsmen, grooms, and standard-bearers, in addition to characters representing the ancient rulers of the city; the Captain of the People, the « Podestà », the Banner-bearers, the Chief Magistrate, the « Biccherna » Superintendents and others.

Outstanding, among the characters mentioned above, for their beauty and bright colours, are the performers of the 17 « Contrade »; each is composed of 19 members.

20

At the rear of the procession comes the «Carroccio» on which is hoisted the «Palio», the prize awaiting the winner of the horse race.

The most spectacular part of this procession is the flagplay, in which the standard-bearers of the various « contrade » throw their banners into the air, with rapid, fanciful movements, exhibiting great skill, adroitness and a wealth of imagination.

Thus we come to the central, most-awaited part of the festival - the horse race - for which the Piazza del Campo is particularly well suited. The horses of ten «contrade» take part in it, and the winner is presented with the Pallium (from which the festival takes its name),that is to say, a pennant with a picture of the Virgin.

In this way, the most ancient traditions of the city's past come to life again for a few hours in their full flavour, transforming and almost obliterating the daily life of modern Siena.

Top right: *Under starter's orders.*
Bottom right: *The horses rush headlong in a mad dash to win the Palio.*

Top left: *The noble art of flag-waving.*

Top right: *General view of the Piazza del Campo.*

Left: *The Standard-bearer of the She-wolf District.*

Right: *Victory Dinner.*

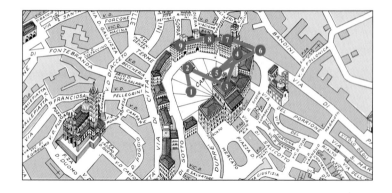

1 PIAZZA DEL CAMPO

Siena's history and the events that accompanied and characterised it find their material expression in the Piazza del Campo, which for this very reason has come to be the centre, and at the same time the symbol, of the life of the city.

Situated approximately at the intersection of its three hills, it shows obvious signs of this position: it is semicircular in shape, sloping towards the centre.

Its paving, which dates from 1347 is of bricks, laid in herring-bone pattern (the people of Siena were in great demand for the paving of streets and squares in many places); it is divided up into nine sections (recalling the Government of the Nine), by means of longitudinal strips of white stone.

This particular shape and design give the general impression of a shell; in fact, here we have one of those instances in which the difficult conditions of the terrain are overcome and even lead to the creation of real masterpieces of technical skill and, above all, of art.

This accounts for the picturesque attractiveness of this square which, to its own beauty and that of the palaces surrounding it, adds the fascination of the medieval atmosphere which still seems to cling to it.

2 GAIA FOUNTAIN

On the side opposite the Town Hall, in the central part of the Campo, stands the **Gaia Fountain**, built between 1400 and 1419 by Jacopo della Quercia (1374-1438), one of the most important Sienese sculptors of this period. His art displays, together with the Gothic elements current up till that time in the Sienese artistic tradition, a clear appreciation of classical plastic and spatial values, thus heralding the coming Renaissance style, and, above all, constituting one of the earliest examples of that calm dignity and harmony

Piazza del Campo.
Gaia Fountain.

which were soon to dominate architecture, sculpture and painting. The original sculptures of the Gaia Fountain are at present in the Town Hall, having been replaced, in 1868, in order to save them from the ravages of time, by other, not faithful, reproductions by Tito Sarrocchi.

Starting from the left, the sculptures represent:

The Creation of Adam; Wisdom; Hope; Strength; Prudence; Angel; Madonna with Child; Angel; Justice; Charity; Temperance; Faith; The Expulsion of Adam and Eve from the Garden of Eden.

The Fountain, fed by an aqueduct some 25 Kms long, dating from 1344, was inaugurated in 1414: from that day it has been called «Gaia» (Gaiety) in memory of the great festivities which marked the occasion.

3 TOWN HALL

The **Town Hall** is in perfect harmony with the Square, and, with its three wings facing in different directions, seems to unite in its embrace the particular structure of the whole area in front of it.

Its building started in 1288 and went on till 1320.

Later additions were made to it: in 1327 the prison and, about the middle of the 14th century, the Great Council Hall. Another storey was then added to the two side wings: this addition is clearly shown by the small hanging arches above the three-mullioned windows. It was once the seat of the Podestà and is now occupied by the Municipality.

Exterior

The Palace is the clearest example, and certainly one of the most elegant, of the Tuscan Gothic style.

The lower part is of stone with a series of arches called «Sienese» because of their original shape: they consist of a pointed arch subtending a flattened one.

The second and third storeys, like the rest of the Palace, are faced in brick and are rythmically broken up by a series of very elegant three-mullioned windows with slender columns of white marble.

The fourth storey, which is higher than the two side wings, is marked by a pair of mullioned windows at the sides and by a large copper disc in the centre, with the name of Jesus Christ (the symbol of San Bernardino), painted and adorned in 1425 by Battista di Niccolò di Padova and by Turino.

4 THE TORRE DEL MANGIA

To the left of the Town-Hall the beautiful Torre del Mangia rises to a height of some 102 metres. It is called after the nickname of its first bell-ringer, the Mangiaguadagni or Mangia. It was built by Minuccio and Francesco di Rinaldo of Perugia (1338-48).

It is almost entirely faced with brick; the fine top of stone, which also contains the belfry, was designed by Lippo Memmi in 1341.

The big bell, or Sunto (so called because it was dedicated to Maria Assunta), is by Girolamo Santoni and Giovan Battista Salvini (1666). The clock is a restoration of the one by Giovanni da Milano.

Admission to the Tower, allows you to enjoy a wonderful view of the Sienese countryside and the neighbouring hills.

Town Hall.

5 THE PIAZZA CHAPEL

At the foot of the **Torre del Mangia** stands this original Chapel, built by the people of Siena in gratitude for their escape from the plague in 1348.

It was designed by Domenico di Agostino, who started it in 1352, it was finished only in 1376 by Giovanni di Cecco. Between 1468 and 1470 it was embellished with arches in the Renaissance style by Antonio Federighi. It was further ornamented by niches and statues added in later periods. The iron gates are of the 14th century, by Conte Lello Orlandi and Pietruccio di Betto.

Interior: an interesting fresco by Sodoma:

- *The Virgin with Saints and the Eternal Father* (1539).

At the right end of the Palace there is a COLUMN with a Corinthian capital. Above it:

- *The She-Wolf suckling the twins*, by Giovanni and Lorenzo Turino (1429-1430).

Interior of the Town Hall

Here are housed works of great interest.

In the Hall there are:

-two *she-wolves* in stone commonly attributed to Giovanni Pisano;

-*Moses* by Antonio Federighi;

-fresco by Sano di Pietro (1406-1481) depicting *Sienese Saints and Blessed Souls*. In the rooms used as premises for municipal offices there are some outstanding works to be admired: *The Coronation of Mary between Saints Bernardino and Catherine* by Sano di Pietro, the *Resurrection* (Sodoma, 1537), works by Lorenzo Veneziano, del Salimbeni and a fresco attributed to Simone Martini.

On the first floor the **Museum** proper is housed.

Hall: a fine *Madonna and Child* by Ambrogio Lorenzetti is kept here.

Hall of the Globe: its name derives from a large map depicting the territory of Siena by Ambrogio Lorenzetti but which has now disappeared. In this room are also displayed two of the greatest masterpieces of Italian art:

- **The Majesty:** this dates from 1315. The dampness of the walls has caused progressive deterioration: Simone Martini himself restored it in 1321.

The fresco shows the *Madonna enthroned between Angels and Saints*, a favourite subject of artists of the time, and hence often painted. Simone Martini, however, brought a new touch and a new artistic sense to so hackneyed a subject. The flowing, delicate and harmonious Gothic line finds in Simone Martini an artist who handles it with great sensitivity, displaying in this painting a mastery and a balance never attained before. The linear style so typical of Gothic art is evident in every face and emphasises every drapery in this composition, yet it never degenerates into heavy arabesques or affectation; it only serves to harmonise and soften the whole, thus expressing the serene mysticism of the subject.

- **Guidoriccio da Fogliano**. This painting dates from 1329 and is another of Simone Martini's masterpieces. This time the subject is not religious: it commemorates the feat performed by the General Guidoriccio da Fogliano, victor of the siege of Montemassi. Once again, the artistic result is remarkable: in a landscape barely indicated and with scarcely any variety in outline and colour, there stands out, right in the centre, impressive in its isolation, the figure of the general, vibrant with colour of various hues.

Below this fresco are to be seen:

Civic Museum - Hall of the Globe: Guidoriccio da Fogliano.
The Maestà (Simone Martini).

31

- *Majesty* by Guido da Siena, dating from the first half of the 13th century, or according to others, from the second half.
- *San Vittore* (Sodoma).
- *S. Ansano baptizing* (Sodoma).

Among other works worth noticing in this room we would mention; above the arches:
- *Battle of the Sienese against the Florentines at Poggio Imperiale* (by Giovanni di Cristoforo and Francesco di Andrea, 1480).
- *Battle of the Sienese led by Giordano Orsini against the English Company of Cappello, led by Niccolò da Montefeltro at Asinalunga* (a work of the latter half of the 14th century, by Lippo Vanni).

On the pillars:
- *S. Catherine of Siena* (a fine painting by Vecchietta).
- *S. Bernardino* (Sano di Pietro, 1460).
- *Blessed Bernardo Tolomei* (Sodoma, 1533).

We now turn to the right into the
Peace Room: this was where the Government of the Nine held its meetings. It takes its name from the large representation of Peace in one of the frescoes with which it is adorned (the fresco depicting «The effect of Good Government in town and country»).

Since the room was the seat of government of the rulers of the City, it contains an important and significant cycle of frescoes dealing with the functions that were exercised here. Moreover, these frescoes constitute the most important and serious work of the Sienese painter Ambrogio Lorenzetti, who completed them between 1337 and 1339. The subjects are:
- **Allegory of Good Government.**
- **The effect of Good Government in town and country.**
- **Allegory of Bad Government.**
- **Effect of Bad Government in town and country.**

The allegorical subjects which dominate most of these frescoes, were certainly not very congenial to the artist: their attraction lies mainly in the atmosphere of fairyland in certain landscape backgrounds of the countryside round Siena, and still more in that glimpse of city life which we get in the bold perspective of these streets and squares of Siena with its many towers.

We now proceed to the
Room of the Pillars: among the most important works in it we record:
- *S. Bernardino preaching in Piazza del Campo.*
- *S. Bernardino driving the devil out of a woman.* These two paintings by Neroccio di Bartolomeo Landi are on the two sides of a wooden board.

In a glass case in the middle of the room are displayed:
- an iron *coffer.*

Peace Hall: Effects of Good Government (Ambrogio Lorenzetti).

- *the bell* of the Church of S. Cristoforo, which was rung on the day of the Battle of Monteaperti.
- 2 *Crucifixes* of the 12th century.
- various coats of arms, bonzes and furnishings.

Antechapel: here you will see a St. *Christopher* by Taddeo di Bartolo and, also by the same artist, the depictions of illustrious personages of ancient Rome and mythological figures.

Chapel: this is separated from the Antechapel by a wrought-iron grille, an elegant piece made in 1437 by Niccolò di Paolo and Giovanni di Vito. Inside the Chapel:
- Holy *Family*, a canvas by Sodoma (1536), on the altar carved by Marrina (1476-1534).
- *fine chandelier* in the Gothic style, of gilt wood, 1370.

- exquisite wooden *choir stalls*, by Domenico di Niccolò, called Niccolò dei Cori by reason of this masterpiece and other similar ones (1363-1453?).

It consists of 22 inlaid and carved stalls with subjects taken from the **Creed**, executed in a style still reminiscent of the Gothic, between 1415 and 1428.

The vault is completely covered with *frescoes* by Taddeo di Bartolo with sacred subjects.

Cardinals Room, where are displayed:
- Madonna *with Child* by Guidoccio Cozzarelli (1450-1516).
- *a Crucifix* of the 14th century.

Concistorial Room, with an interesting marble **doorway** by Bernardo Rossellino. The inlaid jambs are by Niccolò dei Cori. On the

Peace Hall: Allegory and Effects of Bad Government.

Peace Hall: Effects of Good Government in the city.

Hall of the Priors: Naval battle between the Venetians and the Imperials. (Spinello Aretino).

Bottom: The Town Hall Chapel.

Bottom right: Hall of the Priors. Alexander III entrusts the sword to the Doge of Venice.

vault, very fine frescoes by Domenico Beccafumi (1486-1551), with representations of. *Justice, Concord, Patriotism, heroic deeds from Greek and Roman history.*

On the walls of the Room: 18th century Gobelin *tapestries* and others of Florentine manufacture.

The Power Room, also known as **The Priors Room:** so called because it was the seat of the Government; it is divided into two parts by a large archway. The frescoes which completely cover the walls were painted in 1407 by Spinello Arentino (1352?-1410 with subjects from the *life of Pope Alexander* III.

On the vault; representation of 16 Virtues, by Martino di Bartolomeo (1408).

The door on the right, of inlaid wood, is the work of Niccolò dei Cori, while the wooden bench along the entrance wall is by Barna di Turino.

Monumental Room, or **Room of Victor Emanuel II:** this is completely decorated by 19th century Sienese artists. Here are represented all the decisive events which, under Victor Emanuel II,

---

Hall of Pillars - "San Bernardino preaching in the Campo".

Hall of Pillars - The miraculous liberation of Genuzia from the demon during the funeral rites of San Bernardino.

led to the unification of the Kingdom of Italy, and the principal figures who contributed to this. The following are some of the artists who worked on this room: Alessandro Franchi, Tito Sarrocchi, Pietro Aldi, Amos Cassioli, and others.

Through the door on the left, we reach the rooms surrounding the Courtyard of the Podestà: part of the **Town Museum** is housed here, with a most interesting and complete collection of *coins* (including seals, medals of all periods and the series of Sienese coins), ceramics and engravings.

Loggia: with 4 large arches and a view over the territory of Siena.

Along the walls of the Loggia the *original sculptures* by Iacopo della Quercia *of the Gaia Fountain* have been placed.

The Meetings Room, or **della Signoria,** where there are two canvases by Amos Cassioli.

The Town Hall contains yet other halls used to house the Town Museum: here are kept paintings, prints, geographical maps and

39

various documents concerning the territory and the history of Siena. The **Courtyard of the Podestà**: this was built of brick, like the Town Hall, in 1325. A row of pillars supports large arches, surmounted by an order of most delicate three-mullioned windows.

The courtyard is decorated with the *coats of arms* of former Podestà. From the courtyard we ascend the Torre del Mangia.

The Piazza del Campo is surrounded by a series of palaces: in virtue of a law of 1297, these were supposed to have three-mullioned windows in order to conform to the style of the Town Hall. However, for the most part, this regulation was not observed, but in spite of this, the harmony and beauty of the whole did not suffer.

6 PICCOLOMINI PALACE

Begun in 1469, probably to the design of Bernardo Rossellino, it was built by Pietro Paolo del Porrina da Casale. The building is the finest and most important example of Sienese Renaissance architecture.

Piccolomini Palace: Tax collector and taxpayer (attributed to Ambrogio Lorenzetti - 1340).

Piccolomini Palace: Mystical weddings of Saints Catherine of Alexandria and Catherine of Siena (D.Beccafumi - 1548).
The restored Government keeps the citizens in check (unknown author -1385).

Piazza del Campo.

Its lines, very similar to those of Rucellai Palace at Florence (the work of Leon Battista Alberti), and of the Piccolomini Palace at Pienza (the work of Bernardo Rossellino), possess the dignified elegance of the best Florentine Renaissance architecture. The building consists of two storeys, separated and emphasised by elegant cornices; the whole surface is faced with smooth ashlar and accurately divided by two rows of refined and simple mullioned windows. The building is adorned by wrought iron brackets and coats of arms. The palace now houses the **Record Office**, which may be reached across the courtyard. It contains a collection of important historical documents dealing with the City of Siena: parchments, administrative documents, bulls and various files of correspondence. The most interesting of these exhibits is the collection of *Painted Tablets* of the Bic-cherna (tax collector's office). These were formerly used as covers for the books dealing with the Municipal Administration. On each of these tablets are depicted coats of arms and portraits of the persons who took part in the administration of the current year, or various scenes of the political and religious life of the city.

The Tablets, covering the very long span from 1258 to 1659, were painted by the different artists who worked at Siena in the various periods: Pietro and Ambrogio Lorenzetti, Giovanni di Paolo, Sano di Pietro, Taddeo di Bartolo, Vecchietta, Francesco di Giorgio Martini, and Domenico Beccafumi.

7 CHIGI-ZONDADARI PALACE

This is a 1724 reconstruction of an older building.

8 SANSEDONI PALACE

which, with its great bulk, its tower, formerly much higher and more imposing, and with its curved frontage to follow the line of the Piazza del Campo, is very similar to the Town Hall. The row of delicate three-mullioned windows also harmonises well with the whole architecture of the Square. The building dates from 1216, but was enlarged and remodelled in 1339 by Agostino di Giovanni.

9 LOGGIA DELLA MERCANZIA

Between 1417 and 1429, the building is an important example of the transition period between Gothic and Renaissance style. The three large arcades on the façade are clearly Renaissance in style, but the niches and statues adorning it are distinctly Gothic. It was designed by Sano di Matteo, but later remodelled in the 17th century when the upper floor was added.

The back part which looks onto Piazza del Campo was designed by Niccolò dei Cori. As regards the sculpture, we would mention the statues placed in the tabernacles of the pillars, and, among these, the two by Vecchietta:
- St. Peter.
- St. Paul.

The two marble benches at the sides of the Loggia are by Federighi (1464) and Urbano da Cortona.

⚜

Sansedoni Palace.

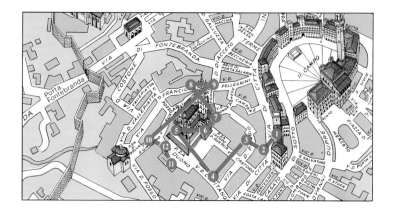

1 PALAZZO CHIGI-SARACINI

It was built in the 14th century, but later enlarged and then restored.

The building, slightly and elegantly curved to follow the contour of the ground and of the street, consists of two storeys (the first of stone, the second of brick), with two orders of three-mullioned windows.

On the left it is flanked by a tower from which, it is said, Cerreto Ceccolini followed the various stages of the Battle of Montaperti, passing on the news to the people of Siena from time to time.

In 1930, at the wish of Count Chigi-Saracini, the palace was made the seat of the **Chigi Music Academy**, which in a short time, became one of the most important for advanced musical studies.

The **Interior** contains art treasures, donated to the Academy together with the palace, by Count Chigi-Saracini. Among these, we would mention the very interesting collection of musical instruments, some of which are exceedingly rare.

In addition to the Concert Hall, we advise a visit to the **Gallery** with its valuable collection of works of art:
- Madonna with St. John, by Sassetta.
- St. Martin, Madonna and Saints, likewise by Sassetta.
- Madonna, by Vecchietta.
- Madonna, by Sano di Pietro.
- Madonna enthroned, with Saints and Angels (Sandro Botticelli).
- Madonna enthroned, with Saints and Angels (Spinello Aretino).
- Portrait (Sebastiano del Piombo).

We further mention works by Francesco di Giorgio Martini, Sodoma, Perugino, Beccafumi and Matteo di Giovanni.

44

Chigi-Saracini Palace.

2 PICCOLOMINI PALACE OR PALAZZO DELLE PAPESSE

Thus called because it was built for Caterina Piccolomini, the sister of Pope Pius II.

The building, begun to the design of Bernardo Rossellino, was erected between 1460 and 1496; it later underwent restorations, such as that by Augusto Corvi in 1864. It is in the Renaissance style, with the characteristic façade of ashlar, rough below and smooth higher up. However, it departs from this style, like almost all 15th century palaces at Siena, as compared with those at Florence, inasmuch as it adopts artistic elements taken from other styles, especially from Gothic.

In the case of this building - but this is also true of others - these consist of the two orders of mullioned windows adorning the upper floors.

3 PALAZZO MARSILI

It dates from the middle of the 15th century, although executed at the height of the Renaissance period, the building still displays some Gothic features, such as the three orders of three-mullioned windows in the façade.

As far as Piazza Postierla the **Torre Forteguerri house** stands.

4 PALAZZO DEL CAPITANO DI GIUSTIZIA

This very fine building was so called because it was the seat of the Chief Magistrate; later it belonged to the Grottanelli, Pecci and finally to the Piccolomini families.

It dates from the 13th century, when it was built in a typically Gothic style, as shown by the Sienese arches on the ground floor and the mullioned windows on the upper floor. Subsequently, in the 15th century, it was remodelled by Luca di Bartolo da Bagnocavallo into a Renaissance-type building. Still later, in the 19th century, it was restored to its original aspect.

In the Interior, the *Courtyard* of the Capitano di Giustizia is interesting, with an outside stairway leading directly to the upper floors.

5 CATHEDRAL

Which stands on a very ancient temple dedicated to the Goddess Minerva, later replaced by a small church. The building shows clear traces of the artistic influences to which it was subjected during the long period of its construction. It was in fact begun in 1229, and completed only towards the end of the 14th century. In 1264, it was finished as far as concerns the central part of the Basilica and the cupola.

Between 1284 and 1299, Giovanni Pisano, who was called in by the Cistercian monks of San Galgano, built the façade, although unfortunately he did not go beyond the lower part.

The whole of this area, consisting of three large arches, is clearly in the Romanesque style, imbued with the classical feeling for elegant proportion and harmonious dignity, but at the same time enlivened by a marked plastic relief due to the distribution of light and shade, which was such a feature of this 13th century artist.

When the façade was left unfinished at the first stage, it was decided to prolong the apse along the downward sloping ground of Valle Piatta. This work was entrusted to Camaino da Crescentino.

However, the Cathedral underwent still further enlargement. Siena's ever increasing prosperity and expansion led to plans for another enlargement: according to this project, the present Church would have become only the transept of a larger building placed transversally to it, majestic and imposing in its dimensions and architecture.

The part thus planned was begun in 1339, and its execution entrusted first to Lando di Pietro, and later to Agostino and Domenico di Agostino, but the overbold and, above all,

Exterior of the Cathedral.

too costly scheme was very soon abandoned.

It was then decided to complete the building of the old Cathedral, by finishing the remaining parts. In 1382 the apse was completed, while at the same time the vaults of the centre aisle were raised. In 1376, it was decided to go on with the façade, and the work was entrusted to Giovanni di Cecco. This upper part shows the most obvious signs of the changes of purpose and style which occurred in so long a span of time. This part is in the Gothic style (similar to the façade of the Cathedral of Orvieto, built by Lorenzo Maitani of Siena), in complete contrast with the Romanesque of Giovanni Pisano, but nevertheless merging with it thanks to the subtle distribution of the richly animated parts.

Thus it is that, in spite of these vicissitudes and the simultaneous presence of the Romanesque and of late Gothic styles, the beauty of the Cathedral remains unimpaired.

EXTERIOR OF
THE CATHEDRAL

The Façade is of white marble, delicately contrasted with pink Siena and dark green Prato stone; as already mentioned, the whole of this part is divided into two areas.

The lower one, by Giovanni Pisano in the Romanesque style, consists of three enormous arches (the centre one round and the two side ones slightly pointed), with three finely decorated doorways.

This part, with its delicate classical elegance, is adorned with the statues made by Giovanni Pisano himself, they glow with vitality and with an intimate lyricism which serves to express the artist's intensely felt dramatic spirituality.

Most of the originals are now preserved in the Cathedral Museum, to save them from the ravages of time.

The upper part of the façade by Giovanni di Cecco, is one of the clearest and finest examples of that decorated Gothic which had already found magnificent expression in the Cathedral of Orvieto by Lorenzo Maitani. The

Siena Cathedral, like the one of Orvieto on which it is modelled, ends in three points, the centre part covered with mosaics executed by the Venetian Castellani in 1877. Their subjects are:
- *The Presentation at the Temple* (mosaic of the left cusp).
- *The Nativity* (mosaic of right cusp).
- *The Coronation of the Virgin* (mosaic of the large central cusp).
Below the central cusp there is a large stained-glass rose window representing
- *The Last Supper* (after the design by Perin del Vaga). Around the rose window are placed 36 busts of *Patriarchs and Prophets*, and in the four triangles between the rose window and the panel surrounding it, pictures of the *four Evangelists*. In the centre top of the panel:
- *The Madonna.*
The originals of these sculptures, made in the 14th century by Corbella, are now in the Cathedral Museum, having been replaced by copies made by Tito Sarrocchi and Leopoldo Maccari in the 19th century.

Right side of Cathedral

It is divided by pillars and large Gothic windows and the whole of its surface is marked by longitudinal bands of polychrome marble, more accentuated in colour than the façade with its two-colour scheme. This marble decoration covers all the rest of the Cathedral.

From this side stretches that part of the New Cathedral left unfinished, which will be described later.

Left side of Cathedral

this cannot be seen, since it has been incorporated in the adjacent Archbishop's Palace.

The main portal of the Cathedral.

THE CAMPANILE

It was built in 1313 to the design of Agostino di Giovanni and Agnolo di Ventura.

It is in the Romanesque style, decorated in marble of two colours, placed horizontally so as to form continuous black and white stripes, thus repeating and completing the colour scheme of the Church. The Campanile is lit by six windows, from one mullion at the bottom to six at the top.

It ends in a point, consisting of a pyramid on a polygonal base, with two smaller and slenderer pyramids at the sides.

THE CUPOLA

It too is very beautiful; it rests on an open gallery, hexagonal in shape, is divided by ribs and culminates in a polygonal lantern.

The Campanile.

INTERIOR OF CATHEDRAL

The interior makes a great impression upon the visitor, being so majestic and at the same time so harmonious through the skilful coordination of the architectural, sculptural and pictorial elements. The brightly coloured marbles completely covering the walls with horizontal bands, the decoration of the vaults with golden stars on a blue ground, and the won-

Interior of the Cathedral.

derful inlaid floor, make this interior particularly inpressive.

The Church is in the form of a Latin cross; it is divided into three aisles by composite pillars surmounted by round arches. When visiting the interior, it is advisable to go around it first to view with attention one of the Cathedral's masterpieces:

The Pavement:

The pavement of the Siena Cathedral is particularly interesting and outstanding. The decoration, in graffiti and inlaid work, was completed at different periods, having been begun in 1372 and finished only in 1562. The various periods of workmanship are indeed easily distinguishable, not only by the style of the artist, but also and above all by the different technique used on each occasion. The oldest graffiti consist of a reproduction of designs by engraving on slabs of marble: the parts engraved were then filled up with black stucco so as to make the picture stand out. This is the most precious part of the pavement and is generally kept covered so as to protect it as long as possible. (It is on view only once a year, from August 15 to September 15). Later another technique was adopted, the designs were reproduced on a dark background to make them stand out more clearly. Still later, the method of inlaying directly was adopted, and coloured marbles were used for this. We start our visit from the entrance wall up to the crossing of the aisles and Transept:

Pavement of central aisle:

1) *Hermes Trismegistus* (Giovanni di Stefano, 1488).
2) *Coat of Arms of Siena* (in centre), Pisa, Lucca, Florence, Arezzo, Orvieto, Rome, Perugia, Viterbo, Massa, Grosseto, Volterra and Pistoia.
3) *Imperial Eagle* (1373).

4) *Fortune* (1504-1506; by Paolo Mannucci, after a design by Pinturicchio).
5) *Fortune and Four Philosophers.*

Pavement of left aisle:

6) *The Libyan Sibyl* (Guidoccio Cozzarelli, 1483).
7) *The Hellespontine Sibyl* (Neroccio di Bartolomeo Landi, 1483).
8) *The Phrygian Sibyl* (Urbano da Cortona, 1483).
9) *The Samian Sibyl* (Matteo di Giovanni, 1483).
10) *The Albunean or Tiburtine Sibyl* (Benvenuto di Giovanni, 1483).

Pavement of right aisle:

11) *The Delphic Sibyl* (Urbano da Cortona, 1482).
12) *The Cumaean Sibyl* (Urbano da Cortona, 1482).
13) *The Sibyl of Cuma* (Giovanni di Stefano, 1482): in this representation, the artist drew his inspiration from the opening lines of Virgil's Fourth Eclogue, as witness the words at the Sibyl's feet. At the top right are recorded the hexameters referred to:
«Ultima Cumaei venit iam carminis aetas; Magnus ab integro saeclorum nascitur ordo. Iam redit et Virgo, redeunt Saturnia regna; Iam nova progenies caelo demittitur alto». (The last age heralded in Cumaean song is come, and the great march of the centuries begins anew. Now the Virgin returns, now Saturn reigns again, and a new race descends from on high).
14) *The Eritrean Sibyl* (Antonio Federighi, 1482).
15) *The Persian Sibyl* (Urbano da Cortona, 1483).

Pavement of right Transept:

16) *The Seven Ages of Man* (1475, original by Antonio Federighi; restored by Alessandro Franchi, 1870).
17) *Faith, Hope, Charity and Religion* (copies made in 1870 by Alessandro Franchi). The originals were by Domenico Beccafumi).
18) *Jephta's Victory over the Ammonites*

PAVEMENT OF THE CATHEDRAL

(Bastiano di Francesco, 1482).

19) *Death of Absalom* (Pietro del Minella, 1447).

20) *The Emperor Sigismund enthroned* (Domenico di Bartolo, 1434).

Pavement of Presbytery:

21) *Moses makes the water gush from the rock* (Domenico Beccafumi, 1525).

22) *The Worship of the Golden Calf* (D. Beccafumi, 1522).

23) *David the Psalmist, David hurling the stone, Goliath struck* (Domenico di Niccolò, 1423).

24) *Moses* (Paolo di Martino, 1426).

25) *Samson's Victory over the Philistines* (Paolo di Martino, 1426).

26) *Joshua* (Domenico di Niccolò, 1426).

27) *Jushua's Victory over the King of the Amorites* (Paolo di Martino, 1426).

28) *Abraham's Sacrifice* (Beccafumi Domenico, 1546).

29) *Prudence* (Marchese d'Adamo and pupils, 1380).

30) *Temperance* (Marchese d'Adamo and pupils, 1380).

31) *Mercy* (Marchese d'Adamo, 1406).

32) *Justice* (Marchese d'Adamo, 1406; very beautiful, probably the reproduction of a design by Ambrogio Lorenzetti).

33) *Fortitude* (Marchese d'Adamo, 1406).

Pavement of left arm of Transept:

34) *Judith decapitates Holofernes; Fighting at the Gates of Betulia* (Antonio Federighi, 1473).

35) *The Slaughter of the Innocents* (Matteo di Giovanni, 1481).

36) *Hercules driven from the Throne* (Benvenuto di Giovanni, 1484).

Pavement underneath the Cupola:

all the panels are attributed to Domenico Beccafumi, and have been partly restored by Alessandro Franchi.

37) *Death of Ahab.*
38) *Elijah's Sacrifice.*
39) *Ahab's Sacrifice.*
40) *Slaying of the False Prophets.*
41) *Rebuke of Elijah.*
42) *Elijah taken up to Heaven.*
43) *Pact between Elijah and Ahab.*

In the rhombs around the above representations:

44) *Elijah raises the widow's son from the dead.*
45) *Elijah annoints Jehu.*
46) *Ardia brings Ahab before Elijah.*
47) *Elijah orders Ardia to bring Ahab before him.*
48) *Elijah fed by the deer.*
49) *Elijay asks the widow for bread.*

Having thus completed the tour of the Church, we now look carefully at the other works contained in it.

Let us first mention the series of 171 *terracotta busts of the Popes*, made in the 15th and 16th century, placed between the arches and vaults. Below these are 46 *busts of Emperors*, starting with Constantine and ending with Theodosius.

Internal Façade

On the pedestals of the central Doorway are bas-reliefs by Ur-

Pavement of left arm of Transept (The Slaughter of the Innocents -Matteo di Giovanni).
Facing: Pavement underneath the Cupola.

bano da Cortona, 1483, showing «Stories from the life of the Virgin».

Near the entrance, close to the first two pillars (on the left and right respectively) are two *Holy Water Stoups* by Antonio Federighi (1463).

Right aisle:

In a niche near the façade:

- *Paul V.* a statue by Fulvio Signorini, 1605.

- *the Tomb of Bishop Tomaso Piccolomini del Testa*, by Neroccio di Bartolomeo Landi (1484-85). On the sides of the Tomb: panels showing the «Life of the Virgin», by Urbano da Cortona.

To the left, we find ourselves beneath the Cupola. It is supported by six pillars, to two of which are attached the two *poles* of the «Carroccio» that was present at the

ARINGHERIIS EQUITIS HYEROSOLIMITAN'

High Altar (*work of Baldassarre Peruzzi 1532*).

Battle of Montaperti. Six columns support gilt statues of *Saints* by Ventura Turapilli and Bastiano di Francesco. Above the pillars and columns runs a false gallery, divided and adorned by 42 small columns and 42 figures of *Patriarchs and Prophets*, by various artists of the 15th century. The Cupola ends in a calotte, above which is the noticeably asymmetric lantern. The lack of symmetry observed in the Church is due to the long period over which its building extended).

Right arm of Transept:

This arm of the Transept, like the left one, has a double aisle, divided by composite pillars. **Chapel of the «Madonna del Voto», or Chigi Chapel:** (marked A on plan). Commissioned by Pope Alexander VII, it was built to the design of Benedetto Giovannelli, between 1655 and 1661. Its architecture, decoration in marble and bronze, and the gilt dome, are a typical example of the Baroque style which dominated the 17th century. Among the works in the

Chapel, we point out:
- The Virgin of the Vow (Guido da Siena, 13th century) (on the altar). Statue by Lorenzo Bernini (1608-1680), showing Angels (these are placed around the Madonna of the Vow). Near the entrance there are two other statues by Bernini, placed in niches: «St. Jerome» and «The Virgin». The statues beside the Altar are by Ercole Ferrata and Antonio Raggi.

We would also mention, to the left of the Altar, a painting by Carlo Maratta (1625-1713): «The Salutation of the Virgin to St. Elizabeth» and in front of the Altar a mosaic («Flight into Egypt»), copied from a painting by Maratta with the same subject. On leaving the Chapel, we find on the right of the Transept:
- Alexander. III, statue by Antonio Raggi (1663).
- Alexander VII, by Ercole Ferrata, 1668 (on the left).
- San Bernardino, by Mattia Preti (on the altar opposite).

Chapel of the Madonna of the Vow.

Chapel of the Blessed Sacrament: contains five interesting bas-reliefs by Giovanni di Truino and Francesco da Imola, representing the «Four Evangelists» and «St. Paul».

Presbytery:

The very fine **High Altar**, 1552, is by Baldassare Peruzzi. Above this Altar are placed:
- Bronze *Ciborium* (a fine work by Vecchietta, executed between 1467 and 1472).
- Two *Angels holding candelabra*, by Giovanni di Stefano (1489).
- *Eight Angels* by Beccafumi, placed on the pillars. In the remaining part of the Presbytery:
- 2 *Choir Galleries*, one by Antonio Barili (high up on right) dating from 1511, the other by Riccio (high up on left), dating from 1550.
- *Bishop's Throne* (left side of Altar): this was made as recently as 1907 by Tito Corsini to a design by Riccio.

Apse:

The niche in the Apse was formerly covered with frescoes by Beccafumi; these have now almost disappeared and have only partly been restored; at the sides of the niche are two frescoes by Ventura Salimbeni: «*Esther before Ahasuerus*» and «*The Jews in the Desert*». The wooden *Choir* on the walls of the Apse is a remarkable work of great beauty; the central stalls were designed by Riccio and carved by Teseo di Bartolino and Benedetto di Giovanni between 1567 and 1570; those at the sides are by Francesco and Giacomo del Tonghio (1362-97). The inlaid work, taken from the Monastery of St. Benedict outside Porta Tufi (now suppressed), are by Fra' Giovanni da Verona. The fine *stained glass rose window* high up reproduces designs by Duccio di Buoninsegna. In it are represented: *Death, the Assumption, the Coronation of the Virgin, the Four Evange-*

lists, and the Patron Saints of Siena.
Sacristy: this is reached through a door on the left of the Apse (see plan). On the left hanging «*Piletta*», a most delicate work of the goldsmith's art, by Giovanni di Turino (1437).

Remains of 15th century frescoes can be seen in the three **Chapels** at the back.

In the **Vestibule**, which is reached through the small Chapel on the left, is a *bust of Pope Alexander VII*, by some attributed to Bernini, by others to one of his pupils.

Chapter House: this is reached through the Vestibule, and contains a collection of portraits of Sienese Popes and Bishops.

Of particular interest the three paintings on wood by Sano di Pietro:

- St. *Bernardino preaching in Piazza del Campo* (1430).
- St. *Bernardino preaching in Piazza S. Francesco* (1440).

- S. *Bernardino* (portrait, 1470).

We return to the Apse and from here proceed to the

Left arm of Transept:

Next to the pillars of the Cupola is the *Pulpit*, by Nicola Pisano and his pupils, such as his son Giovanni Pisano and Arnolfo di Cambio. It is a real masterpiece, completed between 1265 and 1268. It is a few years later than another, simi-

---

The wooden Choir: work executed in marquetry (14th and 15th century).

lar pulpit, also by Nicola Pisano in the Baptistery at Pisa. The one in Siena Cathedral, built six years later than the one at Pisa, is octagonal in shape instead of hexagonal and, above all, the movement of the figures is denser and more complex. It is supported by granite columns, resting alternately on a pedestal and a marble lion. The central column rests on a sculpted group, representing the seven liberal arts: *Grammar*, *Dialectics*, *Rhetoric*, *Philosophy*, *Arithmetic*, *Geometry*, *Music* and *Astronomy*. Above the columns and the Corinthian capitals, the arches close in most elegant trefoil moulding (three-lobed arches), Between the arches, and resting on the capitals, are statues representing the *Sibyls*. The whole upper part of the pulpit is divided into eight panels, separated from one another by statues of Prophets and Angels. Starting from the one near the stairs, these eight faces represent:

1) *The Nativity and Visitation* (imbued with deep human feeling, especially in the gentle figure of the Madonna).

2) *Arrival and Adoration of the Magi.*

3) *Presentation in the Temple; St. Joseph's Dream; Flight into Egypt.*

4) *Slaughter of the Innocents.*

5) *Crucifixion.*

6) *Last Judgement of the Sinners.*

7) *Last Judgement of the Virtuous.*

(The eighth panel is taken up by the stairs leading up to the pulpit, designed by Riccio). We continue

Pulpit by Nicola Pisano - Detail of the Nativity.

Pulpit by Nicola Pisano.

Top:
Detail of the
Flight into
Egypt.

Top right:
Detail of the
Pulpit -
Crucifixion.

Bottom
right:
Details of the
central
column of the
Pulpit.

63

our visit of the Transept, where on the right, we find the *Corner Chapel of St. Ansano* (see on plan). On the Altar: *S. Ansano baptizing the people of Siena* (Francesco Vanni). On the left wall: The large, very fine «*Monument to Cardinal Riccardo Petroni*», by Tino da Camaino (1314-1318). The sarcophagus is supported by four Caryatids, resting on brackets; all three sides have sculptures. On the front:
- *Doubting Thomas.*
- *Resurrection.*
- *Apparition of the Madonna.*

On the sides:

- *The Virgin at the Tomb.*
- *The Meeting at Emmaus.*
Above the sarcophagus is a tabernacle with three points, depicting the «*Madonna and Child*» (centre) and «*St. Peter*» and «*St. Paul*» (sides). In the pavement of the Chapel is the *Tomb of Bishop Giovanni Pecci* (a bronze by Donatello, 1426). Going back to the Transept, we find, placed symmetrically to the statues in the right arm of the Transept:
- *Statue of Pius II* (Giuseppe Mazzuoli, 1698), on the right of the niche.
- *Statue of Pius III* (Pietro Balestra, 1706), on the left of the niche.
On the pavement: a graffito tombstone, 1468. Then follow two Altars, on one of which is placed the wooden Crucifix believed to have belonged to the «Carroccio».
Chapel of St. John the Baptist. The ground plan of this Chapel is similar to that of the Chapel of the Vow in the right arm of the Transept, and it is placed symmetrically to it. Artistically however it is different; it is the work of Giovanni di Stefano, who built it in 1482 in a distinctly Renaissance style. The doorway, of white marble with bas-reliefs and inlaid work, is by Lorenzo Marrina; the gate is by Sallustio Barili.
Among the important works in it, we point out:

- *stuccoes and decorations* by Caponeri and Cosimi Lucchi (1596).
All along the lower fascia of the Chapel, starting from the left, we find:
- *Alberto Aringhieri* (portrait painted in 1504 by Pinturicchio).
- *S. Ansano* (marble statue by Giovanni di Stefano, 1487).
- *St. John the Baptist* (bronze statue by Donatello, made by the master in his last period. Together with his «Mary Magdalene» in the Baptistery at Florence, it is the most important example of the power of expression achieved by the artist at this final stage of his art).
- *The Beheading of St. John the Baptist* (another painting by Pinturicchio, completed by Rustichino).
- *St. Catherine of Alessandria* (statue by Neroccio di Bartolomeo Landi and pupils, 1487).
- *Alberto Aringhieri* (another portrait by Pinturicchio).
On the upper fascia of the Chapel:
- *St. John the Baptist in the Desert* (Pinturicchio).
- *The Baptism of Christ* (Rustici).
- *St. John the Baptist preaching* (Pinturicchio).
- *St. John the Baptist in Prison* (Cesare Maccari).
In the centre of the Chapel:
- *Baptismal Font* (Attributed to Antonio Federighi): It is octagonal in shape, and on its eight faces are carved 6 Stories of Adam and Eve, Samson and the Lion, and Hercules and the Centaur.
On leaving the Chapel, we find in a niche immediately to the right the «*Monument to Marcantonio Zondadari*», by Giuseppe and Bartolomeo Mazzuoli.

Left Aisle:

at the fifth arch is the *Piccolomini Library*. Two arches form the entrance: in the right-hand one is placed an altar with bas-relief depicting «*St. John the Evangelist*», by Vecchietta in the left one is the *bronze door* of 1497, a work by

Chapel of St. John the Baptist.

Ormanni. In the lunette above the entrance is a fresco painting with the «*Coronation of Pius III*» by Pinturicchio.

Interior of the library; this is one of the most important interiors of the Renaissance. It was built for Cardinal Francesco Piccolomini in 1495, who was later to become Pope Pius III, to house the books of his uncle, Pius II. It consists of a single rectangular room, and its walls are divided by pilaster strips and entirely covered by a cycle of fresco paintings. These are by Pinturicchio (1454-1518), who depicted in them the main events in the *life of Pope Pius* II, in a simple, lively style and in an essentially decorative manner. In the centre of the hall, on a beautiful Renaissance stand, there is the roman copy of the marble group of the:

- *Three Graces*, belonging to the school of Praxiteles, going back to the III century BC.

In order to follow the cycle in chronological and logical sequence, we start from the end window on the right:

1) *The young Enea Silvio Piccolomini leaving for the Council of Basle to act as secretary to Cardinal Capranica.*

2) As Ambassador of the Council at the Court of King James of Scotland. (The fresco shows a good sense of perspective and picturesque views).
3) He is crowned poet by the Emperor Frederick III
4) He is sent as Ambassador by the Emperor Frederick III to Pope Eugene IV.
5) As Bishop of Siena, he presents to Frederick III, at Porta Camollia, his promised bride, Eleanor of Portugal.
6) He is elected Cardinal by Pope Callixtus III.
7) He is elected Pope.
8) Pius II at the Congress of Mantua proclaims the Crusade against the Turks.
9) Pius II canonises St. Catherine. (In this beautiful fresco, the Pope is sitting in the centre, surrounded by his Cardinals, with the Saint's body lying at his feet. In the lower part of the picture, lay persons who are portrayed, among whom the portraits of Raphael and of Pinturicchio himself, on the left can easily be discerned).
10) Pius II goes to Ancona to urge the departure of the Crusade (this is one of Pinturicchio's finest fresco paintings). The ceiling of the Library, likewise richly decorated, has in the centre the Coat of Arms of the Piccolomini Family, and all around panels with mythological and allegorical representations, by pupils of Pinturicchio. Very elaborate «grotesque» decorations complete the adornment of this most beautiful room. The majolica pavement incorporates in its design the coats of arms of the Piccolomini Family. Apart from the frescoes, also note some illuminated antiphonaries arranged along the walls; the miniatures are by a number of artists, including Liberale da Verona, Girolamo da Cremona, Sano di Pietro, Pellegrino di Mariano, and others. Over the entrance door, there is a bas-relief depicting «Adam and Eve driven from the Garden of Eden», considered by some to be a copy of an original by Jacopo della Quercia,

by others attributed to the artist himself. On leaving the Library, we continue along the left Aisle, and immediately come to a sculptured group by a follower of Michelangelo, Bandino Bandini: the group depicts «The Risen Christ between two Angels».
- Piccolomini Altar (by Andrea Bregno); it consists of a large niche in which is placed the Altar, surrounded by other, smaller niches, in which are placed statues of; St. Gregory, St. Paul, St. Peter, St. Pius. All these are by Michelangelo, although artistically they are not very important. The «Madonna» in the niche at the top has recently been attributed to Jacopo della Quercia.

Piccolomini Library: Miniated choir-books.
Bottom: the "Three Graces" a famous sculpted group of the Roman epoch.

6 THE NEW CATHEDRAL

As already mentioned, in 1339 a magnificent Cathedral was planned at Siena in honour of the Virgin, to be erected by making use of the part of the Cathedral which was already in existence. This would have become the Transept of the new and more impressive nave of the Cathedral which was to have taken up the whole area at present covered by the Piazza Jacopo della Quercia.

First Lando di Pietro, and later Domenico di Agostino, were engaged in building it, up to 1355.

Of this immense project, there remains today the whole of the large right aisle, consisting of five wide arches, as well as another three on the left side. There also remains the so-called «Facciatone», that is to say the great façade which was never finished.

In the closed arches of the right aisle is the "Opera Metropolitana" Museum.

❧❧❧

7 «OPERA METROPOLITANA» MUSEUM

Begun in 1870, other collections of works of art were later added to it. It mostly contains sculptures and paintings connected with the Cathedral. There are many pieces of great artistic and documentary interest. These are spread over three floors and divided into various rooms. Each work is appropriately catalogued and bears the date and origin.

A list of the most prestigious pieces follows:

- **Madonna and Child, Saint Anthony Abbot and Cardinal Casini kneeling**: an outstanding piece in high relief from the mature years of Jacopo della Quercia. It belonged to the Siena Cathedral; it was then lost and found again in 1972;

-**statues** by Giovanni Pisano including Moses, the Prophets, the Sibyls, all originating from the façade of the Cathedral;

the **Maestà**, masterpiece by Duccio da Buoninsegna.

- The *Maestà*, a magnificent painting, created between 1308 and 1311 for the High Altar of the Cathedral of Siena, where it remained until 1505. Later the front part was separated from the back

Facing: *Lower hall of the Museum.*

Top right: *Opera Metropolitana Museum. Madonna and Child, Saint Antony abbot and Cardinal A. Casini (Jacopo della Quercia).*

part (which was also painted, as we shall see), and they were placed in the Chapel of S. Ansano and the Chapel of the Blessed Sacrament in the same Church respectively. In 1878 they were transferred to the «Opera Metropolitana» Museum.

This masterpiece, once much larger, consisted of the great central canvas, depicting the Maestà, a series of smaller paintings on wood with the «7 Stories of the Virgin» at the sides, and a predella with «Stories of the Virgin and Christ». The back part, painted completely with «Stories of Christ's Passion», which was separated from the front part in the 18th century, is displayed in the same room. The small paintings on wood from the sides, and the predella were likewise detached from the main painting, and are almost all placed in various museums in different parts of the world, while

Top: Moses by
Giovanni
Pisano.

Right: Abacuc
by Giovanni
Pisano.

Facing:
Altar-piece of
the Maestà by
Duccio di
Buoninsegna.

one piece was lost.

Duccio's great art is immediately revealed in the central part of the painting: «*The Madonna enthroned between Angels and Saints*». The various stylistic components of Duccio's art here combine in marvellous harmony: on the one hand his Byzantine manner, seen in the general disposition of the group in a frontal aspect and in the gold ground of the picture; on the other hand, the Gothic refinements and linear elements (the cusp above the Madonna the richly modulated drapery of the Madonna's cloak). However, the general orchestration of the painting goes beyond the individual style of Duccio's art: the solemn preciousness of the whole is redeemed by the slow, gentle movement of the heads of the Saints and Angels, while their faces and postures are made human by a serene and intimate lyrical note.

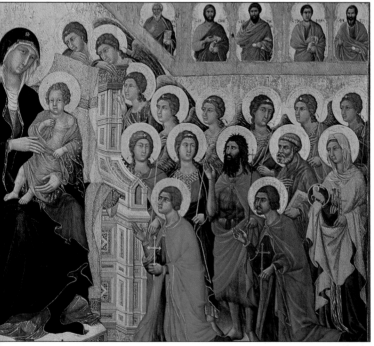

The back of the Maestà consists of 26 panels (placed to the left of the entrance), showing «Stories of Christ's Passion»: here Duccio's art is no longer seen in the solemnity of the whole and the mysticism of the composition, but in the details of the events depicted and in the clear expressiveness of the gestures and postures. In each panel, the landscape merges with the figures and accompanies their movements; the clear and dazzling colour transfigures every dramatic action, as if immobilising it in time, thus conferring upon it an essentially lyrical tone. (Starting to examine them from the lower section):
- The Entry into Jerusalem (this and the «Crucifixion» are the largest panels).

The Maestà: Crucifixion by Duccio di Buoninsegna.

The large-eyed Madonna (anonymous Sienese artist).

- Christ washing the Disciple's Feet.
- The Last Supper.
- Christ's words after the Supper.
- The Pact of Judas.
- Christ's Agony in the Garden of Gethsemane.
- The Capture of Christ (one of the finest pictures, where the drama is brought out by the broken and undulating line).
- The Denial of Christ.
- Christ in the presence of Anna.
- Christ before Caiaphas.
- Christ smitten.
- Christ in Court.
- Christ before Pilate.

Upper section

- Christ in the presence of Herod.
- Christ before Pilate for the second time.
- The Scouriging.
- The Crown of Thorns.
- Pilate washing his hands.
- The Road to Calvary.
- The Crucifixion (undoubtedly one of Duccio's most dramatic creations, which marvellously succeeds in bringing out the full

73

tragedy of the event: the Cross stands out high and clear on a compact background; beneath, the onlookers crowd to the sides, almost as if to leave the way open to Christ).
- *Descent from the Cross.*
- *The Placing in the Tomb.*
- *The Holy Women at the Tomb.*
- *Descent into Hell.*
- *Appearance to Mary Magdalene.*
- *Appearance at Emmaus.*
In the same room we find:
- *The Birth of the Virgin* (Pietro Lorenzetti, 1342, one of the artist's most beautiful and important works).
- Madonna di Crevole (Duccio), brought here from the Church of S. Cecilia at Crevole.
- Reliquary of the head of S. Galgano (attributed to Lando di Pietro: in silver gilt, of very fine and elegant Gothic workmanship, dating from the 13th century).
- *Crucifix* of gilt wood (by Giovanni Pisano).

Third Floor

Large Room: we single out from the main works:
- «*The large-eyed Madonna*» from the first half of the 13th century, made by an anonymous Sienese artist. The painting on wood was originally on the High Altar of the Cathedral of Siena, where later Duccio's Maestà was placed. It is of great importance, both from the artistic point of view, since it influenced a large part of Sienese art, and from the historical point of view, as the people of Siena went to pray before this picture on the eve of the famous Battle of Montaperti.
- **The Blessed Agostino Novello and four miracles**: this is one of the most important works by Simone Martini.
- *Saint Paul* by Beccafumi.

8 BAPTISTERY

It was built between 1316 and 1325 and, since it is a continuation of the apse of the Cathedral, it may be almost looked upon as its crypt.

Façade: its design probably goes back to Giacomo di Mino del Pellicciaio. It was begun in 1317 and was continued in 1382 in an elegant and dignified Gothic style, but the upper part was never completed. To some extent, it follows the design and colour scheme of the Cathedral, but the overall effect is calmer and more severe. There are three doorways in the lower part, with a pronounced cusp over the middle one. Over the doorways is a very delicate row of small pensile arches. Three slender ogival windows crown the upper part of the façade. In front of the doorways, the somewhat damaged pavement shows pictures concerning the function of the Baptistery:
- *Birth of the child* (left), by Bartolomeo di Mariano, 1450.
- *The child is taken to the Baptistery* (centre).
- *The Baptism* (right).
The last two are by Antonio Federighi, 1451

Interior of Baptistery: this is by Camaino da Crescentino and Tino da Camaino (1325). It consists of a rectangular room, in which two pillars form three aisles with ogival arches and vaults. In the end wall is a small polygonal apse.

The vaults of the Baptistery are covered with *frescoes*:
Vaults near the façade:
- *The Apostles* (Vecchietta).
Under the arches:
- *Prophets and Sibyls* (Vecchietta).
Other Vaults:
- *The Articles of the Creed* (School of Vecchietta).
Right Lunette:

Baptistery of **St. John.**

- *Christ in the Pharisee's House* (Pietro Orioli).

Apse:

- *Life of Christ* (the upper part by Michele di Matteo, the lover part by Vecchietta, 1453).

In the centre of the Baptistery is one of the greatest masterpieces of 15th century sculpture, the *Baptismal Font* (1417). It is a great work by Jacopo della Quercia, who made the design and executed some of the sculptures. He cleverly combine the elegance of the linear Gothic with the harmony of the Renaissance style, thus representing the culminating and most significative point of that transition period in Italian art. The base consists of an hexagonal basin from which rises a small pillar, and on top of this there is another hexagonal piece: the *Ciborium*. The Font terminates in a small column surmount-

Baptistery - interior.

ed by the statue of St. John the Baptist, attributed to Jacopo della Quercia or to an artist of his school. We should now note the panels and the other sculptures adorning the Baptismal Font, all of which are artistic masterpieces. We begin with the panel in front of the altar, in the lower part; all these panels are of gilt bronze, with statues between them:

- *Zacharias driven from the Temple* (Jacopo della Quercia, 1417).
- *Justice* (statue by Giovanni di Turino, 1427).
- *The Birth of John the Baptist* (Turini di Sano, 1427).
- *Charity* (statue by Giovanni di Turino).
- *John the Baptist preaching* (Giovanni di Turino).
- *Prudence* (statue by Giovanni di Turino).
- *Baptism of Christ* (Lorenzo Ghiberti, 1427).
- *Faith* (statue by Donatello).
- *John the Baptist taken prisoner* (Lorenzo Ghiberti, 1427).
- *Hope* (Donatello, 1428).
- *Herod's Feast* (Donatello, 1427): one of the artist's most significant works, in which the dramatic force which is one of his dominant characteristics, is expressed in the succession and close connection of the perspective lines.
- *Fortitude* (statue by Goro di Neroccio).

Above the basin of the Font is the Ciborium, likewise hexagonal.

Baptismal Font: Baptism of Jesus (Lorenzo Ghiberti).

Baptismal Font: the Angel announcing to Zacharias the birth of the Baptist (Jacopo della Quercia).
Bottom: Herod's feast (Donatello).

In the niches of its six faces it shows:
- 5 *Prophets* (Jacopo della Quercia).
- *Madonna and Child* (Giovanni di Turino).

The *Angels* between the faces are by Donatello and Giovanni di Turino.

9 PALACE OF THE MAGNIFICO

On the right side of Piazza San Giovanni stands this building, erected for Pandolfo Petrucci, Seigneur of Siena. It was built in 1508 and is attributed to

---

Baptismal Font: *Capture of the Baptist* (*Lorenzo Ghiberti*).

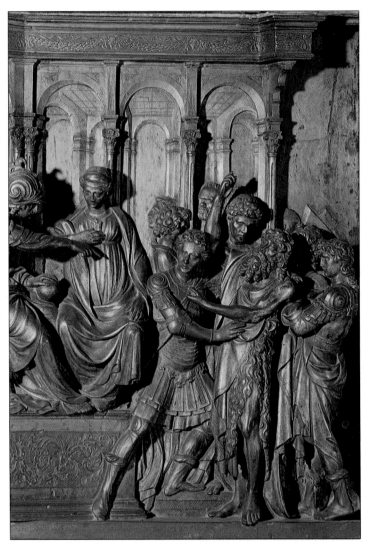

Domenico di Bartolomeo di Piacenza, but the design is perhaps by Giacomo Cozzarelli.

The frescoes and the many valuable works of art which once adorned this palace, are now either lost or displayed in Various Galleries, among them the Picture Gallery of Siena.

꧁꧂

10 HOSPITAL OF SANTA MARIA DELLA SCALA

The building, erected for the Canons of the Cathedral, dates from the 13th century, and has kept some features of that period, such as the elegant row of mullioned windows in the façade.

Interior: In the internal rooms there are sculptures and paintings of great merit.

1st Vestibule: here we admire an interesting *wooden ceiling* in the Renaissance style, by Guidoccio d'Andrea. Moreover, on the left, there is the *tomb of Jacopo Tondi*, by Giacomo Cozzarelli.

2nd Vestibule: this is reached by the door on the right of the 1st Vestibule. Among other particularly interesting works, there is:

- *The Meeting of St. Joachim with St. Anne*, by Domenico Beccafumi (1512).

- *Infirmary and Pilgrim's Hall* (St. Catherine used to nurse the sick here): this is specially interesting for a cycle of 15th century *frescoes*, unique of its kind, not only as a document of the costumes of the period, but also as an illustration of the hospital work carried on here. Starting from the door and proceeding towards the right, we note:

- *Acts of Charity* (Domenico di Bartolo, 1440).

- *Reception and feeding of Foundlings; their Weddings* (Domenico di Barto-

lo, 1440).

- *Supper and nursing of the Sick* (D. di Bartolo).

- *The Wet-Nurses take the Infants into their care and receive their pay* (Giovanni Novesi, 1507).

- *Payment of the wet-nurses' wages in grain* (Pietro di Achille Crogi).

- *The Pope grants the Hospital independence* (Domenico di Bartolo, 1443).

- *The Blessed Agostino Novello hands the Habit to the Rector of the Hospital* (Priamo di Pietro della Quercia, 1432).

- *The Hospital is enlarged* (Domenico di Bartolo, 1443).

- *The Foundlings are taken up to Heaven* (Lorenzo Vecchietta, 1441).

Infirmary of St. Pius: this contains an interesting fresco, representing the «*Blessed Sorore*» (Domenico di Bartolo).

Room of St. Peter: It contains badly damaged frescoes by Vecchietta and by other artists, such as Domenico di Bartolo.

꧁꧂

11 THE ARCHAEOLOGICAL AND ETRUSCAN-MUSEUM

This newly established Museum combines the Bargegli, Petruzzi, Chigi-Zondadari and other collections.

Here are gathered exhibits dating from the remotest periods up to Etruscan and Roman times, discovered in the neighbourhood of Siena.

The exhibits are spread over several rooms. The materials on show are generally grouped in sections (for example the prehistoric section, the topographical section) or on the basis of their territories of origin and excavation areas.

Given the great variety of the pieces on exhibition - which, incidentally, are all catalogued accord-

Above: Hospital of Santa Maria della Scala.
Bottom: Interior of the Church of SS. Annunziata.

ing to the epoch to which they belong or the place where they were found - we will mention only the collections or the finds of greater importance.
The prehistoric section exhibits materials dating back to the epochs which stretch from the palaeolithic to the Iron Age: it consists for the most part of casts, weapons, handmade articles, ornaments, vases as well as vegetal residues and bones buried in the tombs and in the cavities of Monte Amiata, Pitigliano and Cetona.
The topographical section covers the greatest number of rooms and the exhibits are grouped on the basis of their territory of origin.
Of great importance are those originating from the area of Chiusi which include both stone instruments, as well as bronze objects, Canopi, buccheros, terracottas, urns: the pieces are often decorated with mythological scenes.
The territory of Chianciano, Monteriggioni, Sferracavalli, the farm of Santo Polinari and the Val d'Elsa have thrown up large quantities of finds: apart from vases and cinerary urns, there are a number of very varied funeral collections.
There are several very fine sarcophagi: some stand out for their beautiful decoration and bas-relief generally showing hunting scenes. There is an interesting sarcophagus known as the Muse Chigi sarcophagus (originating from the villa Chigi near Siena).
Among the finds of greatest importance are the Etruscan and Roman ones and in particular a very fine *Head of Seneca*: this is a copy of a Greek original which portrays a personage fairly well known in his time and probably refers to Seneca. There is a precious *amphora* with depictions - these are drawn in black - of a warrior on his chariot surrounded by Satyrs and Maenads: it dates back to the 6th century B.C. The archaeological Museum also houses a coin collection: it contains collections of coins originating from various epochs and various regions, including Lazio, Umbria and the Marche.

12 CHURCH OF SANTA MARIA DELLA SCALA OR OF THE SS. ANNUNZIATA

It dates from 1252; in 1466 however, it was rebuilt by Guidoccio di Andrea.
Interior: this consists of a single nave, raised in the Presbytery. The wooden ***ceiling*** with painted panels is worthy of note.
Among the other important works, we mention:
- 2 inlaid *organs*, by Baldassare Peruzzi, of which the one on the right is especially beautiful.
- Wooden *Choirstalls* running the length of the Apse (Ventura Turapilli).
- *The Risen Christ* (on the High Altar), a bronze statue by Vecchietta (1476).
- *Piscina* (basin) with attractive effects of perspective, by Sebastiano Conca.

The Sacristy contains a large and interesting collection of treasures.

The Oratory of St. Catherine of the night

Through the Oratory (with fine wooden choir stalls of the 15th century), we reach the **«Cappella dello Sposalizio»** (Chapel of the Mystic Marriage), and then the **Cell of St. Catherine of Dirna**. Here there is an interesting terracotta by Vecchietta, representing **«St. Catherine asleep»**.

The Cathedral and the Archbishop's Palace.

In the adjoining Sacristy there is a «Madonna and Child with St. John the Baptist and St. Andrew», by Taddeo di Bartolo.

The Confraternity of the Flagellants contains a «Madonna with St. Peter and St. Paul», by Alessandro Casolani (on the Altar); «The Last Judgment» (in the Sacristy), attributed to Martino di Bartolomeo and a «Pietà» (in the lunette), by Sano di Pietro.

13 ARCHBISHOP'S PALACE

The building forms almost an integral part of the Cathedral.
It was built between 1718 and 1723, and is an attempt to imitate the Gothic style of the Cathedral, in order to be in harmony with it.
In its interior it houses a wonderful Madonna del latte by Ambrogio Lorenzetti.

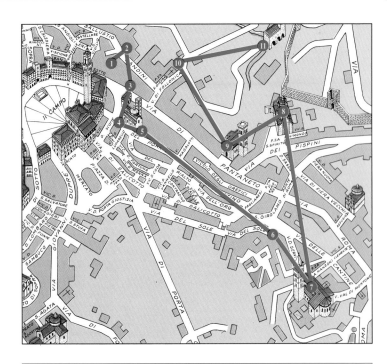

1 UNIVERSITY

Which dates from the 13th century. In the Interior, in the courtyard, there are two interesting monuments:

- *Monument to the students who fell at Curtatone* (bronze group by the sculptor *Raffaele Romanelli*, 1892).

In the Portico:

- *Tomb of Niccolò Aringhieri* (lecturer in Law at the University), the work of an unknown Sienese artist. (XIVth century).

2 CHURCH OF SAN VIGILIO

Which in successive periods belonged to the Camaldolites, the Jesuits and the Vallombrosans, and underwent several reconstructions. The façade is of the 18th century, the work of Antonio Meucci.

The Interior is in the Baroque style, with panelled ceiling, painted by Raffaele Vanni. On the altars in the nave are interesting canvases by Volterrano (1611-1689), Mattia Preti (1613-1699) and Algardi.

3 LOGGE DEL PAPA

They have three large arcades with cross vaults in the Renaissance style. The building, intended by Pius II for his relatives, was erected by Antonio Federighi, and decorated by Francesco di Giorgio Martini.

4 CHURCH OF SAN MARTINO

A work of the late Renaissance, it was built by Giovan Battista Pelori in 1537, while the façade, dating from 1613, is the work of Giovanni Fontana. The **interior** has one nave only, like most of the Siena churches, and richly carved marble altars adorn the walls. Among the works of art here we would mention:

Right wall:
- *The Circumcision*, painted by Guido Reni in 1640 (2nd altar).
- *The Martyrdom of St. Bartholomew*, by Guercino. The marble frame is by Lorenzo Marrina (3rd altar).
Opposite the altar: five statues: *Madonna with Child* (by Jacopo della Quercia); *St. Peter*, *St. Bartholomew*, *St. John*, *St. Anthony the Abbot* (all by pupils of Jacopo della Quercia).

Right Arm of Transept:
- *Tommaso da Villanova*, statue by G. Mazzuoli (on the altar).
- *The Conception* (by G. Mazzuoli) (opposite the altar).

High Altar: this is the work of Lorenzo Marrina; the statues are by G. Mazzuoli.

Apse:
- a beautiful *stained glass window* by Pastorino de' Pastorini, showing «*St. Martin*».
- remains of badly damaged frescoes in the ogival Chapel to the left of the apse.

Left wall of nave:
3rd altar: «*The Nativity*», painting by Domenico Beccafumi.
The marble altar is by Lorenzo Marrina.
2nd altar: two wooden statues of the 15th century.
1st altar: «*St. Ivo*», by Raffaele Vanni.

5) ARCICONFRATERNITA DELLA MISERICORDIA

Founded in 1250 by Beato Andrea Gallerani. In the Oratory there are some interesting works:
- *The Virgin Mary* (wooden statue by Lorenzo Marrina).
- *Gabriel* (by Lorenzo Marrina).
In the Council Chamber: coffin headpieces by Cozzarelli and Beccafumi.

6 CHURCH OF SAN GIROLAMO

Which dates from the 14th century. The interior has a single nave and contains a:
- *Coronation of the Virgin* (Sano di Pietro, 1465).
- *Works by Cozzarelli and Marrina*.
In the CLOISTER, interesting frescoes were recently discovered.

7 CHURCH OF SANTA MARIA DEI SERVI

The original Basilica was built in the 13th century, but later underwent reconstruction and transformation which continued until the 15th-16th century.

The adjoining Campanile is likewise of the 13th century, but was entirely restored in the 20th century; it is in the Romanesque style, richly embellished by four orders of windows (with one to four mullions, from bottom to top row).

The **Façade** is simple and unadorned, with a single doorway and a rose window (indications of another can be discerned on the wall). The **Interior** is in great contrast with the rough and bare aspect of the exterior. Here a dignified and harmonious Renaissance style has been adopted, the design of which is attributed to Baldassare Peruzzi.

The ground plan is in the shape of a Latin cross, divided into three aisles by columns supporting round arches.

The Renaissance style does not continue into the Transept and Apse, which are in the Gothic style. Near the entrance we note: a *Crucifix* of the 14th century and a *Holy Water Stoup* of the 13th century.

Numerous works of art embellish

Basilica of Santa Maria dei Servi.

the church and, among the many, we will mention only the most important.

Right Aisle:

- 2nd altar: *Madonna del Bordone,* by Coppo di Marcovaldo (1261). 5th altar: «*The Slaughter of the Innocents*» by Matteo di Giovanni (1491); «*The Adoration of the Shepherds*» by Taddeo di Bartolo; «*Madonna and Saints*» by Matteo di Giovanni.

- *Madonna with Child,* by Duccio di Bonaventura.

- *The Slaughter of the Innocents,* by Pietro Lorenzetti.

- *Madonna del Popolo* by Lippo Memmi.

- *Herod's Feast* (Pietro Lorenzetti).

- *The Death of* St. *John the Evangelist* (P. Lorenzetti).

- *Madonna of the Belvedere* by Giacomo di Mino del Pellicciaio (1363);

- *Annunciation* by Francesco Vanni;

- *Coronation of the Virgin* by Bernardino Fungai.

In addition there are works by Cozzarelli and Girolamo del Pacchia.

ORATORY OF THE HOLY TRINITY

It contains works by Giuseppe Nasini, Sano di Pietro, Neroccio di Bartolomeo Landi.

PALAZZO DI SAN GALGANO

In the Renaissance style as far as concerns the main body of the architecture and the characteristic facing with smooth ashlar, but the two simple and restrained rows of mullioned windows are Gothic.

8 CHURCH OF THE HOLY SPIRIT

Built in the Renaissance style, it dates from 1498, while the marble doorway, by Baldassare Peruzzi, was built in 1519. The cupola is the work of Giacomo Cozzarelli.

The Interior is in the shape of a Latin cross, with a cupola at the crossing of the two arms, and one nave only. **Ist Chapel, «degli Spagnoli»**; this is entirely decorated with paintings and frescoes by Sodoma, one of the most important of Sienese artists, who was particularly influenced by the painting of Leonardo.

We mention the following pictures:
- S. *Niccolò da Tolentino and the Archangel Michael* (altar).
- *The Virgin hands the habit of the Dominican Order to St. Alfonso* (lunette).

The following frescoes are worthy of note:
- St. *Sebastian* (left wall).
- St. *Anthony the Abbot* (right wall).
- S. *Giacomo da Compostella* (at the top).

Right wall: near the entrance wall we see a **«Crib»** of coloured terracotta, the work of Fra Ambrogio della Robbia (1509).

2nd Chapel: a fine wooden statue of San *Vincenzo Ferreri*, by Giacomo Cozzarelli.

3rd Chapel: «*The Coronation of the Virgin*» by Domenico Beccafumi.

4th Chapel: this contains works by Francesco Vanni and Ventura Salimbeni.

Apse:
- *Pentecost*, fresco by Giuseppe Nasini.
- *Four Saints*, by Rutilio Manetti (1608) - (on the pillars of the high altar).
- Two *choirs*.

Left Wall:
3rd Chapel:

- Wooden *Crucifix* by Sano di Pietro.
- Two wooden statues representing St. *Jerome* and «*The Madonna*», generally attributed to Giacomo Cozzarelli.

2nd Chapel: this contains another wooden statue by Cozzarelli, representing St. *Catherine of Siena*.

Ist Chapel: on the altar a work by Matteo Balducci (16th century): «*The Virgin Mary*».

On leaving the Church, we note in the square in front of it, the **Fontana dei Pispini,** 1534.

9 CHURCH OF ST. GEORGE

The original church dates from the 13th century, when it was built to commemorate the Battle of Montaperti (1260).

The Campanile, of the same period, is Romanesque in style, and has remained in its original state. The church, however, was reconstructed in 1471 by Giovanni di Pietro da Cremona.

In the Interior: Tomb of Francesco Vanni.

10 CHURCH OF S. GIOVANNI BATTISTA DELLA STAFFA

A 13th century building which was almost entirely rebuilt in 1563 by Giovanni Battista Pelori, and restored in the 19th century.

In the Interior are works by Raffaele Vanni, Rutilio Manetti, Ventura Salimbeni, Antonio Federighi and Paolo di Giovanni di Fei.

11 FOLLONICA FOUNTAIN

This is one of the most famous of the many fountains in Siena, and, with its three large pointed arches, certainly one of the most beautiful. It was built in the 13th century.

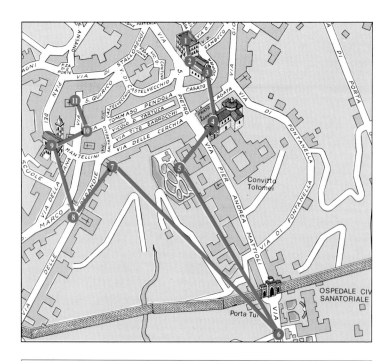

1 PALAZZO BUONSIGNORI

A very fine building in the Gothic style, with two rows of mullioned windows and crowned by a crenellated top. It dates from the 14th-15th century; in it is housed the

NATIONAL PICTURE GALLERY

This contains a collection, in chronological order or by artists, of all the Sienese paintings from the 12th to the 16th century. The collection was started by Abbé Giuseppe Ciaccheri in the 18th century; later, enlarged by new acquisitions, it became State property in 1930. The collection of paintings is spread over more than 30 rooms: all the works carry titles, the date and the artist's name, as well as other useful indications for a better understanding of the work or its history. As it is impossible to give an exhaustive list of the copious collection, a list of the most important paintings follows.

-*Victory*, a partial sculpture of the Roman era: it was part of a sar-

National Picture Gallery.

cophagus;
-*bas-reliefs* by Giovanni Turino;
-*cartoons* of the pavement designs in the Cathedral;
-*frontal* with a depiction of the Redeemer, a fine work of 1215;
-*Transfiguration*, a fine frontal by Guido da Siena;
-*Painted cross* with six stories of the *Passion*, one of the first Sienese paintings (12th century);
-*the Baptist enthroned*, Sienese school of the 12th century;
-two *Madonnas and Child and Saints*, Duccio da Buoninsegna;
-*Our Lady of Mercy*, by Nicolò di Segna;
-*Madonna of the Franciscans*, by Duc-

cio da Buoninsegna, one of the Master's finest works;
-*Madonna and Child* by Bartolo di Fredi (there are various works by the same painter on exhibition including a beautiful *Adoration of the Magi*, a vivacious painting full of charm. It was painted between 1370 and 1380);
-*Madonna and Child*, one of the masterpieces of Simone Martini;
-*City by the sea and Castle by the lake*: an important work by Ambrogio Lorenzetti. It consists of two small panels originating from the Municipal Archive. Their importance, apart from their fine execution, is tied to the fact that they are the first

works with a naturalistic subject;

-*Madonna and Child and Saints*: this is the title of various works by Ambrogio Lorenzetti, among which stands out the one showing the Saints and the Doctors of the Church;

-*Annunciation*, a beautiful painting by A. Lorenzetti;

-*Stories of the Carmelite order*: an outstanding work by Pietro Lorenzetti which belonged to the Carmine church;

-various works by Paolo di Giovanni Fei (his *Birth of Mary and SS. Jacopo, Catherine of Alexandria, Bartholomew and Elizabeth of Hungary* is a great masterpiece), Michelino da Besozzo, Giovanni di Paolo (polyptych of *Our Lady of the Assumption*, altar step with depictions of the *Presentation of Mary to the Temple*, the *Crucifixion* and the *Flight into Egypt*), Matteo di Gio-

---

National Picture Gallery: Madonna of the Franciscans (Duccio di Buoninsegna).

National Picture Gallery: *The Adoration of the Magi* (Bartolo di Fredi - 1370-1380).

vanni, Sassetta (his *Last Supper* is very fine, an important work in Sienese painting), Sano di Pietro (there are a vast number of his paintings in the collection, all of great artistic merit), Neroccio, Luca di Tommé;

-*Madonna and Child and Saints Jerome and Bernardino*, maybe Neroccio's most delicate and beautiful creation (15th century);

-*Holy Family with San Giovannino*, one of the most beautiful works

by Pinturicchio. The painting was executed during his stay in Siena on the occasion of the decoration of the Piccolomini Library;

-*Saint Elijah and the plague victims*: it is one of Rutilio Manetti's best creations (16th century);

-**Nativity**, a work by Sodoma, one of his most important paintings (1503).

Various works by the artist are on exhibition among which stand out **Christ at the Column** (of great spir-

National Picture Gallery: Flight into Egypt (Giovanni di Paolo).
National Picture Gallery: Nativity (Andrea di Bartolo).

National Picture Gallery: Annunciation (Ambrogio Lorenzetti - 1344).
National Picture Gallery: Holy Family with San Giovannino (Pinturicchio).

National Picture Gallery: The Madonna commends Siena to Callisto III (Sano di Pietro).

itual nobility and stylistic finesse, which was part of a larger work executed between 1511 and 1514 for the Convent of St. Francis in Siena), the *Deposition from the Cross*, an early work of 1413, the *Descent of Christ into Limbo* and the *Prayer in the Garden*, works of 1525 which are part of frescos;

-works by Beccafumi (16th century): numerous precious paintings by the artist are on exhibition. Among the many the ones which stand out for their interpretative skill are: *Saint Catherine receives the stigmata*, the *Stories of Saint Catherine*, the *Birth of the Virgin* and the *Descent of Christ into Limbo* (1530-35);

-the works of many other artists are on show, both Italian and foreign, in the last section of the Gallery: Riccio, Brescianino, Vasari, Andrea del Sarto, Girolamo del Pacchia, Lotto (his *Nativity* is outstanding in its sweetness), Padovanino, Rosselli, Vanni, Paris Bordone, Vecchietta;

-a fine *Portrait of Elizabeth of England*, probably executed by Federico Zuccari;

-*Saint Jerome* is one of Dürer's most expressive works, 1514.

2 THE HOUSE OF PIA DEI TOLOMEI

A simple but elegant building, in which lived the famous Pia dei

National Picture Gallery: City on the sea (Ambrogio Lorenzetti).

Tolomei, mentioned by Dante in his «Purgatory».

3 CHURCH OF SAN PIETRO ALLE SCALE

The present 18th century church does not preserve any features of the original ancient building dating from the 13th century.

In the Interior (with only one nave, which also has been completely rebuilt), we can admire some important works, such as: -The Flight into Egypt, by Rutilio Manetti (1621), on the High Altar, one of his most powerful creations.

In addition, there are works by Ambrogio Lorenzetti, Sano di Pietro, Giovanni di Paolo, and others.

On leaving the Church, we contin-

National Picture Gallery: Portrait of Queen Elizabeth of England (Federico Zuccari).

ue along Via San Pietro to its end, beyond the **Porta dell'Arco**, till we reach the

༺ﾟﾟ✿ﾟﾟ༻

4 CHURCH OF. ST. AUGUSTINE

The original building dates from the 13th century, but it underwent various alterations in the 15th and 16th century (the latter at the hands of Luigi Vanvitelli)..

The present **Tolomei State Boarding School** once the Convent of St. Augustine, is joined on to the Church and partly conceals its façade. The Interior of the Church was also completely transformed by Vanvitelli in the 18th

century. It was a single nave.
Right Wall: we mention among the most important works:
- 2nd Altar: *Crucifix with Saints* (Perugino, 1506).
Right Transept; this leads to the *Piccolomini Chapel.*
Right Wall: «*The Blessed Agostino Novello, and Stories of his Life* (Simone Martini); on the Altar: «*The Epiphany*», masterpiece by Sodoma;
on the end Wall: «*Maestà*», by Ambrogio Lorenzetti; left Wall: «*Slaughter of the Innocents*», by Matteo di Giovanni, 1482.
We return to the Church and proceed to the **Presbytery:** this is enriched by four Chapels, two on the right and two on the left.
-2nd Chapel: majolica floor by Pietro and Niccolò Mazzaburroni (15th century). - High Altar: «*Tabernacle*» of polychrome marble, by Flaminio del Turco; «*Urn*» with the relics of the Blessed Agostino Novello.
- 2nd Chapel on the left of the Presbytery: «*The Temptation of St. Anthony*» by Rutilio Manetti.
- **Left Wall of nave.**
- 3rd Altar: «*Baptism of Constantine*», by Francesco Vanni (1586).
- 2nd Altar: «*The Immaculate Conception*», by Carlo Maratta (1671).
On leaving the Church, we find near Piazza Sant'Agostino, usually called Prato di Sant'Agostino, close to the little Church of S. **Mustiola della Rosa** the Academy of Fisiocritici.

※☆☆※

5 ACADEMY OF THE FISIOCRITICI

founded towards the end of the 17th century. It contains the Museum of the Academy of the Fisiocratici with interesting collections, divided as follows: **Museum of Geology and mineralogy**: this extends over the Ground Floor, the Cloister and the 1st Floor. In it are displayed interesting collections of fossils, mammals and molluscs, found in the environs of Siena. We further mention: rocks and various specimens of many kinds of soil, likewise from the neighbourhood of Siena. **Zoological Museum**: its rich collection of fauna occupies eight rooms on the Ground Floor.

※☆☆※

6 THE CEMETERY OF THE MISERICORDIA

reached by Via Pier Andrea Mattioli (between the Church of Sant'Agostino and that of S. Mustiola della Rosa), after passing through Porta Tufi, which dates from the 14th century. The Cemetery contains some important works of sculpture and architecture, of which we mention the most noteworthy only:
- *Metz Chapel*, with an «*Angel of the Resurrection*», by Tito Sarrocchi.
- *Pannocchieschi Chapel*, with paintings by Sarrocchi.
- *Piccolomini Chapel*, with works by Alessandro Franchi and Cesare Maccari.
- *Venturi-Gallerani Chapel*, works by Alessandro Franchi.
- *Bichi-Ruspoli Chapel*: it contains a «*Pietà*» by Giovanni Dupré (1866).

※☆☆※

7 THE CHURCH OF ST. NICCOLÒ AND ST. LUCIA

It was originally built in the 14th century, but was altered in the 16th. We mention in the Interior: the vault, richly decorated by Ventura Salimbeni, Francesco Vanni, and others, as well as works by Giacomo Cozzarelli.

8 THE CHURCH OF ST. PETER AND ST. PAUL

It dates from the 17th century and was built by Flaminio del Turco. It is in the shape of a Greek cross, that is to say, it has two arms of equal length.

In the Interior:
- Altar on right: «Madonna», 13th-14th century.
- High Altar: «Coronation of the Virgin» (Brescianino).
- Altar on left: «Conversion of St. Paul» (Astolfo Petrazzi).

9 THE CHURCH OF SAN NICCOLÒ DEL CARMINE

This Church, with the adjoining Campanile and the Cloister with its fine frescoes, was built in the 14th century, as shown by the architecture in general, although it was partly rebuilt in the 16th century, perhaps by Baldassare Peruzzi. The part most in line with the original construction is the Interior: it consists of a single nave with a ceiling of painted trusses.

Right Wall:
- Adoration of the Shepherds (Ventura Salimbeni).
- 2nd Altar: «St. Michael», by Domenico Beccafumi.
- beyond the 2nd Altar: remains of a fresco by Ambrogio Lorenzetti.
- Chapel of the Blessed Sacrament: particularly noteworthy the marble Altar by Lorenzo Marrino, and above it, the two works by Sodoma: «The Birth of the Virgin» and «The Eternal Father».
- Madonna of the «Mantellini», 1240.
Presbytery:

(behind the Altar).
Left Wall:
- 3rd Altar: «The Assumption», by Girolamo del Pacchia.
Almost opposite the Church stands the **Palazzo Pollini**, designed in the 16th century by Baldassare Peruzzi.

10 THE ORATORY OF ST. ANSANO

Which once was the Chapel of the Prison of S. Ansano (IXth century). Nearby is a Tower (the **Rocchetta**), perhaps dating from Roman times.

11 THE LITTLE CHURCH OF S. QUIRICO AND S. GIULIETTA

As we see it now, it is a 16th century building, but it was originally erected in the 13th century. In the Interior are works by Ventura Salimbeni, Francesco di Vanni and others.

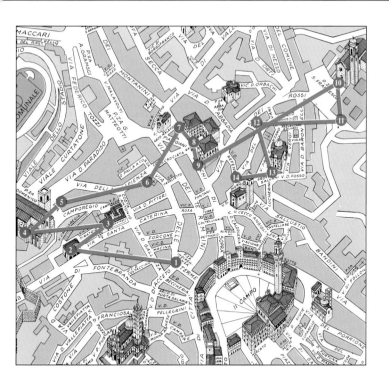

1 ACCADEMY OF THE ROZZI

Close to Piazza della Indip.we see the **Academy of the «Rozzi»**, dating from the 16th century, and the **Theatre of the «Rozzi»**.

～∞◎∾～

2 THE BRANDA FOUNTAIN

It is of very ancient origin, being already known in the 11th century.

It looks almost like a small fortress, leaning against the rock on which stands the Basilica di San Domenico. The Fountain is faced with brick, and has three large open ogival arches, surmounted by three closed ogival arches. Small pensile arches and crenellations complete its decoration. Its present appearance is that given to it in 1246 by Giovanni di Stefano, although it later underwent some alterations.

～∞◎∾～

3 THE HOUSE AND SANCTUARY OF ST. CATHERINE

This was the house of the Saint (1347-80, Patron Saint of Italy since 1939 and one of the most ardent and active personalities of her time. Her mysticism and unshakable faith make her one of the highest examples of the Christian religion, and at the same time an important figure also in the realm of history: we have only to remember that it was she who persuaded Pope Gregory IX to move the seat of the Papacy back from Avignon to Rome in 1337.

The House of St. Catherine and its surroundings comprise today the group of buildings known as the Santuary of St. Caterina.

Via della Galluzza.

Branda Fountain.

THE SANCTUARY OF ST. CATHERINE OF SIENA

It consists of the Upper Oratory (St. Catherine's kitchen), the Lower Oratory (her father's workshop), the «Oratory of the Camera» (The Saint's bedroom), and the Church of the Crucifix (the garden of the House).

Interior: we go straight up to the kitchen, now made into the **Upper Oratory.** The remains of the old

House of Saint Catherine.

hearth (into which the Saint fell as a child, without hurting herself) can still be seen. The floor is also worth noticing (it is generally covered up to avoid further damage); it consists of over 3000 *small terracotta tiles, which* were almost entirely replaced

The coffered wooden ceiling, like-wise restored (Riccio, 1594) is also very fine.

Along the walls beautiful Renaissance stalls.

On the Altar: a painting by Bernardino Fungai, of «*The Stigmata* of St. Catherine».

Above each of the 17 stalls is a picture: beginning from left of the Altar, they are as follows:

1) Christ showing St. Catherine the Cross she had given to a poor man (pupil of Sodoma).

2) S. Ambrogio Sansedoni (Gaetano Marinelli, 1865).

3) The Saint comforting two men condemned to death (Lattanzio Bonastri, 1589).

4) The Communion of the Saint (Pomarancio).

5) Healing of a man possessed by devils (Pietro Sorri).

6) The Blessed Giovanni Battista Colombini (Alessandro Casolani).

7) Christ exchanging His Heart with that of St. Catherine (attributed to Francesco Vanni).

8) The Holy Spirit illuminating St. Catherine (Rutilio Manetti).

9) Canonisation of the Saint (Francesco Vanni).

10) St. Catherine receiving the Crown of Thorns (Francesco Vanni).

11) St. Catherine has a vision of Christ at the Column (Rutilio Manetti).

12) The Blessed Andrea Gallerani (Francesco Vanni).

13) St. Catherine persuades the People of Rome to obey Pope Urban VI (Alessandro Casolani).

14) Gregory IX leaving Avignon to return to the Holy See at Rome (Pomarancio).

15) The Mystical Marriage of St. Catherine with Christ (Arcangelo Salimbeni).

16) St. Bernardino (Pietro Aldi).

17) The Saint gives a tunic to a poor man (pupil of Sodoma).

~~~~~

Sanctuary of Saint Catherine of Siena.

THE CHURCH OF THE CRUCIFIX

Through the **Loggetta** (perhaps by Baldassare Peruzzi), we reach the Church of the Crucifix. So called because the 13th century Crucifix, before which the Saint received the stigmata, was placed in it. It has a single nave, decorated in the Baroque style with frescoes on the walls and on the vault, mostly by Giuseppe Nasini. We further note:

- *Apotheosis of St. Catherine* (by Rutilio Manetti), on the Altar.

- *St. Catherine before Gregory IX* (by Sebastiano Conca), on the Altar opposite.

To the right of the entrance to the Church is the **Oratory of the Camera:** (this was her favourite room). It has a coffered ceilin.

On the walls:

- *Stories of the Saint* (by Alessandro Franchi).

- *St. Catherine receiving the stigmata* (Girolamo di Benvenuto).

Next to the Oratory is the **Cell**, in which are preserved various objects belonging to the Saint. We would mention among these, the stone which served her as a pillow.

We go down to the **Lower Oratory**, also called the **Church of St. Catherine in Fontebranda**, or the **Oratory of the Contrada.**

This Church too has a single nave, adorned with paintings and frescoes connected with the life of the Saint.

Among the most important works, we mention:

- *St. Catherine*, wooden statue by Neroccio di Bartolomeo Landi (on the Altar).

- *5 Angels*; by Sodoma (above the Altar).

- *St. Catherine receiving the stigmata* (Gerolamo del Pacchia) (above the Altar, over the fresco by Sodoma). Along the walls of the Church, other frescoes by Gerolamo del Pacchia, Ventura Salimbeni and others.

4 THE CHURCH OF SAN DOMENICO

This Church, in the Gothic style, is very impressive and picturesque, above all where it rises sheer above the Valley of Fontebranda.

It was begun in 1225 and completed, by stages, in 1465. It underwent many alterations in later periods, but has now regained its original aspect, thanks to the restorations made, the last of which was the reopening of the large three-mullioned windows.

By a street to the left we go down to the 14th century **Crypt.**

Interior: with a single nave, in the shape of an Egyptian cross and very impressive:

Chapel of the Vaults: with an interesting *portrait of St. Catherine* (perhaps the only faithful one), made by Andrea Vanni (1322-1414).

Church of San Domenico and interior.

Right Wall of the Church:
- 2nd Altar, «*Madonna*» by Sano di Pietro.
- Chapel of St. Catherine, built in 1488.
Here the *embalmed head of the Saint* is preserved in a reliquary.
The Chapel is almost completely covered with frescoes:
- in the arch of the entrance door: «*St. Luke and St. Jerome*» (Sodoma); «*Blessed Raimondo and Tommaso Nacci*» (Francesco Vanni).
- to the right of the Altar: «*Ecstasy of St. Catherine*» (Sodoma).
- to the left of the Altar: «*Swooning of St. Catherine*» (another masterpiece by Sodoma).
- right Wall: «*The Saint heals a Woman possessed*» (Francesco Vanni).

Church of San Domenico: Saint Catherine (Vanni Andrea).

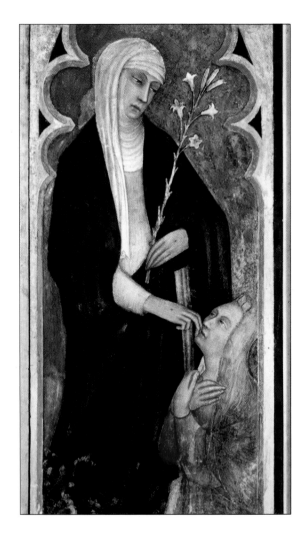

Church of San Domenico: The Saint heals a woman possessed (Francesco Vanni).

Church of San Domenico: Swooning of Saint Catherine (Sodoma).

- left Wall: «*The Saint intercedes in the torment of Niccolò di Tuldo*» (Sodoma).

Continuing along the nave:
- last Altar: «*Nativity*», by Francesco di Giorgio Martini, «*Pietà*» by Matteo di Giovanni (in the lunette).

Right arm of Transept: in the Sacristy and in the 1st Chapel are two

Church of San Domenico: The Saint intercedes in the torment of Niccolò di Tuldo (Sodoma).

works by Sodoma, and in the 2nd Chapel, German students of the 16th and 17th century are buried. The elegant square **Campanile,** dating from the 14th century (ca. 1340), has also undergone considerable alterations: in the 17th century, it was reduced in height, and at the end of the same century, surmounted by a crenellation. Tribune: on the High Altar; a very fine work by Benedetto da Maiano, the *Ciborium* and the *two Angels holding candelabra.*

Left arm of Transept:
- 1st Chapel: «*Madonna and Child*», by Sano di Pietro.
- 2nd Chapel: St. *Barbara enthroned and Saints,* by Matteo di Giovanni. In the lunette, «*The Epiphany*», by the same artist:
- 3rd Chapel: «*Madonna with Child and Saints*», by Matteo di Giovanni.
Left wall: works by Ventura Salimbeni (4th Altar) and Rutilio Manetti (2nd Altar).
To the right of the facade of the Church of San Domenico is the

Nocturnal view of the Cathedral from San Domenico.
Facing: Piazza Salimbeni.

15th century Cloister with recently found frescoes by Lippo Memmi.

✾

5 THE LIBRARY OF THE INTRONATI

Where, in addition to a large number of books of general interest, are preserved *books, pamphlets, incunables* and *manuscripts* of great value. Among the most important items, we mention: illuminated manuscripts, sketchbooks and notebooks of artists, such as Francesco di Giorgio Martini and Giuliano da Sangallo.

✾

6 CHURCH OF SAN PELLEGRINO ALLA SAPIENZA

Built in 1240 over an ancient Chapel dedicated to Our Lady of Mercy, it is now Baroque in appearance.

The Interior is in a plain, severe Baroque style.

Among the most important works we point out the ivory 14th century *Tabernacle* on the right wall.

7 PALAZZO SALIMBENI

Dates from the 14th century and is in the Gothic style, partly re-modelled and enlarged in the 19th century by Giuseppe Partini.

The building has three storeys and a short filight of stairs in front.

On the left, a fine doorway with Sienese arch (a pointed arch supporting a lower one).

There are narrow arcades on the first and third floor, while, on the second, beautiful and elegant three-mullioned windows are inserted between ogival arcades.

A cornice with small arches and a crenellation crown the facade.

8 THE PALAZZO SPANNOCCHI

designed around 1470 by Giuliano da Maiano.
It is in the Renaissance style, faced with smooth ashlar.
On the first floor, a row of rectangular windows, while the upper storeys have two rows of plain mullioned windows.

9 ORATORY OF SANTA MARIA DELLE NEVI

This small building was probably built to the design of Francesco di Giorgio Martini in 1470 and is characterized by its simple Renaissance style. Inside the single naved church is a masterpiece by Matteo di Giovanni, the *Madonna of the snow* (1477) from which the Oratory takes its name. It is a painting of exquisite workmanship and delicate sensitiveness. On the altar step are painted three *Stories from the legend of Pope Liberius*.

10 THE BASILICA DI SAN FRANCESCO

It was designed by Agostino di Agnolo in 1326, and built over a small church which stood on the same site.
It was completed in the 15th century only, perhaps by Francesco di Giorgio Martini. Towards the end of the 19th century it was restored to its original aspect by removing the later additions and repairing the damage suffered: the restoration was carried out under the direction of Giuseppe Partini.

The original Gothic style of the Church is partly respected in the façade which dates from the end of the 19th century and the beginning of the 20th (Vittorio Mariani and Gaetano Ceccarelli).

Interior: the ground plan is in the shape of an Egyptian cross, with a single wide nave, lighted by mullioned windows on the sides and by the large window with four lights in the apse.

Right Wall:
- niche after the 1st lunette: fresco representing *Saints*, a 14th century work of the Sienese school.
- after the door: *tomb of Pia dei Tolomei*.

Oratory of San Bernardino.

Right arm of Transept:
- 2nd Chapel: *tomb of Cristoforo Felici*, by Urbano da Cortona (1462).
- 1st Chapel: *Madonna and Child* (Andrea Vanni).
- **Presbytery**: this has an interesting *stained glass window*, by Zottler of Munich.

Left arm of Transept:
- 1st Chapel: «*The Crucifixion*», by Pietro Lorenzetti (14th century), one of the artist's finest and most dramatic paintings.
- 3rd Chapel: (right wall) «*San Ludovico before Boniface* VIII» by Ambrogio Lorenzetti: (left wall): 14th century frescoes.
- 6th Chapel, or Piccolomini Saracini Chapel, or Chapel of the Blessed Sacrament: with an original floor by Marrina.

Right wall: by a side door, we enter a simple and elegant 15th century **Cloister.**

THE REGIONAL SEMINARY OF PIUS II

built in the 15th century over the ancient Convent of St. Francis. There are some interesting works in the *Seminary Chapel:*
- *Madonna nursing the Child* (Am-

brogio Lorenzetti).
- The Risen Christ (Ambrogio Lorenzetti, in the Refectory).

⚜

11 THE ORATORY OF SAN BERNARDINO

built in the 15th century in honour of San Bernardino of Siena.
In the Interior there are some interesting works:
- The Lower Oratory was decorated by Brescianino and other 17th century painters.
On the Upper Floor we find in the Vestibule:
- Madonna and Child (wooden statue of the School of Jacopo della Quercia).
- Madonna and Child (painting by Sano di Pietro).
- Madonna and Child (bas-relief by Giovanni di Agostino).
Upper Oratory: the ceiling is adorned with decorations by Ventura Turapilli (15th century): the Oratory has works by Sodoma, Beccafumi and Gerolamo Pacchia. Among these, we mention:
By Sodoma:
From Piazza San Francesco we again take Via dei Rossi, until we turn on the left into Via Provenzano Salvani, and then Via del Giglio, where stands the Church of St. Peter Ovile.

⚜

12 CHURCH OF ST. PETER OVILE

dating in its present form, from 1753. However, the façade still retains its original 13th century Romanesque appearance.
The INTERIOR has three aisles.
- 1st Altar on the right: The Annun-ciation, an interesting copy of the original by Simone Martini.
- Altar on left of High Altar: 2 wooden statues («Madonna» and «St. John the Evangelist»), by Domenico di Niccolò dei Cori.
- 1st Altar on left: a fine and interesting «Madonna and Child», by the so-called Master of St. Peter Ovile.

⚜

13 THE CHURCH OF SANTA MARIA IN PROVENZANO

It was designed and built by Flaminio del Turco in 1594, following a previous plan. It is in the late Renaissance Style. The façade of white stone is divided vertically by four pilasters into three sections, and horizontally into two floors by a well marked cornice.
Where the two arms of the Church meet, the slender cupola rises over an octagonal plan, crowned by a high lantern.
The interior is in the shape of a Latin cross and has a single nave. It is in a plain and restrained Baroque style. It contains works by: Rutilio Manetti («San Cerbone», 1st Altar on right), Francesco Vanni («Holy Family», Sacristy).
Il also contains the much venerated 13th century «Madonna di Provenzano», protected by a sumptuous Tabernacle.
One of the two Festivals of the Palio (July 2), is today celebrated in commemoration of her miracles.

⚜

Palazzo Tolomei.

14 THE PALAZZO TOLOMEI

Like most Buildings at Siena, this Palace too is in the Gothic style; moreover it is one of the oldest examples of this style.

Its original part dates from 1205, but it was later remodelled. The exterior has two very high storeys, with two rows of large mullioned windows.

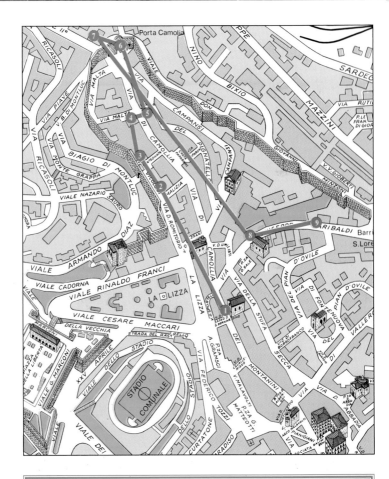

1 THE CHURCH OF ST. ANDREW

Originally built in the Romanesque style, it was completely rebuilt in the 18th century. The Interior, which has a single nave, has on the High Altar an interesting triptych by Giovanni di Paolo, depicting the «Coronation of the Virgin with St. Peter and St. Paul» (1445).

2 THE CHURCH OF ST. BARTHOLOMEW

Dating from the 13th century. It contains the Tomb of Pinturicchio, and in addition:
- *Madonna*, by Sano di Pietro.
- *Madonna and Child*, by Vecchietta.

Porta Camollia, built in '300.
Fortress of St. Barbara.

3 THE CHURCH OF FONTEGIUSTA

The **Exterior:** is in the Renaissance Style. It was built towards the end of the 15th century by Francesco di Cristoforo Fedeli and Giacomo di Giovanni. The fine marble doorway by Urbano da Cortona is worthy of notice.

The **Interior** is built on a square plan, symmetrically divided by four columns, supporting cross vaults, into three aisles.

Entrance Wall:
- *stained glass window* by Guidoccio Cozzarelli.

Right Aisle:
- 1st Altar: *The Visitation*, by Michelangelo Anselmi.
- under the 1st Altar: two small paintings on wood of Apostles (14th century).
- at the corner of the 1st Altar: *Ciborium* by Lorenzo Marrina.
- 2nd Altar: *Our Lord, the Virgin and Saints*, by Francesco Vanni.
- 3rd Altar: *Coronation of the Virgin*, by Bernardino Fungai.

High Altar:
- Marble *Tabernacle* by Lorenzo Marrina.
- *Pietà* (in the lunette), sculpture by Micheli Cioli, who collaborated with Lorenzo Marrina in the High Altar.

Left Aisle:
- *The Sibyl announcing the Birth of Christ to Augustus*, a remarkable work by Baldassare Peruzzi (on the Altar, near the door).

4 THE CHURCH OF ST. PETER ALLA MAGIONE

The building which once belonged to the First Order of the Knights Templars, dates from the 11th century. Its doorway is Gothic, and at the side there is a Renaissance Chapel. The Interior is plain and impressive. Opposite the Church ist the House of Baldassarre Peruzzi.

5 HOUSE OF BALDASSARE PERUZZI

We continue along Via Camollia, which ends at the Gate of that name,

6 PORTA CAMOLLIA

This dates from the 13th century, but was rebuilt in the 17th. It is one of the main gates of the City, famous for the inscription on it «Cor magis tibi Sena pandit» (Siena opens its heart wider to you than this gate).

7 THE ANTIPORTO DI CAMOLLIA

A defensive outpost of the city. It stands outside Porta Camollia, along the city walls.

8 THE CHURCH OF THE COMPANY OF ST. SEBASTIAN

Of the 15th century, rebuilt at a later date.

Interior: 17th century decoration, by Rutilio Manetti and others. We also mention:
- *Wooden Crucifix* which belonged to San Bernardino (High Altar).
- Copy of the Company's Standard (the original is by Sodoma).

9 LA CONSUMA

On leaving the Church, note on the left, the **Casa della Consuma**, mentioned by Dante in Canto XIXX of the Inferno.

Environs of Siena

Convento e Basilica dell'Osservanza - Castello di Belcaro - Castello delle Quattro Torri - Certosa di Pontignano - Montaperti - San Leonardo al Lago - Lecceto - Pieve di Ponte allo Spino - Sovicille - Ancaiano - Cetinale - Castello di Brolio - Lilliano - Villa Cerna - Monteriggioni

CONVENTO E BASILICA DELL'OSSERVANZA

It was originally built for San Bernardino and later rebuilt, perhaps by Francesco di Giorgio Martini.

In the 20th century, it was once more rebuilt after being damaged by bombing, to the original plan.

Façade: In front there is a portico with a sloping roof. The upper part of the facade is divided by two pilasters and surmounted by a large gable.

Interior: it has a single nave, with four chapels at each side.

Left wall:
- 3rd Chapel: *triptych* (by Sano di Pietro), and a reliquary of San Bernardino.
- 4th Chapel: *triptych* (by Sassetta: the attribution to the Master of the Osservanza is better founded).
- on the arch: *terracottas* by Andrea della Robbia.

Right wall:
- 4th Chapel: polyptych by Andrea di Bartolo.
- 2nd Chapel: *terracotta* by Andrea

Basilica dell'Osservanza.

della Robbia, showing the «*Coronation of the Virgin*». Adjoining the Church is the **Aurelio Castelli Museum**, which contains various works, such as paintings, jewellery, illuminated manuscripts, etc.

CASTELLO DI BELCARO

(outside Porta San Marco). It was built in the 12th century and later rebuilt first by Baldassare Peruzzi and then by Partini. The Castle is surrounded by a spacious park with many trees providing deep shade.

CASTELLO DELLE QUATTRO TORRI

It dates back to the 14th-15th century and preserves to a large extent its original structure in which stand out the four soaring towers which give the fortress its name.

CERTOSA DI PONTIGNANO

This Abbey is some 8 Km. from the town.

It consists of three Cloisters and a Church: the 1st Cloister is in the Renaissance Style; the 2nd, smaller one, dates from the 14th century; the 3rd and largest, has some interesting frescoes by Poccetti.

In the Church there are remains of frescoes, among them the «*Stories of the Carthusians*», by Francesco Vanni and Poccetti.

MONTAPERTI

Or, Monteapertaccio, scene of the Battle of that name in 1260. This battle, the glory of Sienese history, the ideal symbol and peak of the political power is attained as an independent city state, was one of the decisive moments in the struggle between Guelphs and Ghibellines.

At that time Siena, which supported the Ghibellines, had extended its dominion over the surrounding

Certosa di Pontignano.

territory as far as Pisa; Florence, which sided with the Guelphs, found in Siena the greatest obstacle to the extension of its political and territorial power.

The Battle of Montaperti, one of the most humiliating for proud Florence, marked the important, although the last, point in favour of the Ghibellines.

Shortly afterwards in fact, in 1269, they were completely defeated, and then Siena too sided with the Guelphs.

On the summit of the little hill of Montaperti now stands a monument, a stone commemorating the victory of Siena.

Colle di Montaperti.
San Leonardo al Lago.

SAN LEONARDO AL LAGO

In the neighbourhood between Belcano and Lecceto, we find another Augustinian monastery of the 12th century. In the interior are frescoes by Lippo Vanni and Giovanni di Paolo. About 14 km. from Siena we reach:

LECCETO

Some 9 Km. from Siena, beyond Belcaro, we find this Augustinian Monastery of very ancient foundation, dating perhaps from the 4th century. Very little remains of the original building; in fact as we now see it, it was almost completely rebuilt in 1317 and again in 1344. The two Cloisters are also very ancient; one dates from the 13th century, the other from the 15th.

PIEVE DI PONTE ALLO SPINO

This religious edifice stands between Siena and Sovicille, along the road which goes from Porta San Marco to Ancaiano. The building, in Romanesque style, has extremely simple lines. The ancient capitals of the interior are of interest as is what remains of the cloister and the Convent.

SOVICILLE

This is a village of ancient origin and is one of the fortresses of the city of Siena which was the site of many of the historical events which affected the Sienese terri-

Castello di Brolio.

tory. The Parish Church of San Lorenzo, even though adapted in the 19th century, still shows part of its mediaeval structure.

⚜

ANCAIANO

This village, of modest dimensions, houses several interesting paintings in the seventeenth-century *Parish*.

⚜

CETINALE

An elegant seventeenth-century construction designed by the architect Carlo Fontana for Cardinal Chigi. The park known by the name of *Tebaide* is outstanding.

⚜

CASTELLO DI BROLIO

Brolio is a term of Longobard origin: the name indicates a woody place.

It is located along the Chianti valley on high ground a little more than 500 metres in altitude: there is a far-ranging view of the green Tuscan hills around.

It is of ancient origin - it dates back to the 9th century - and belongs to the Ricasoli family.

In the 11th century, inside the mighty walls with their pentagonal design, the so-called **Palazzo del Signore** was built. It was then rebuilt in the 15th century after it was destroyed by the Aragonese who had hoped, by taking the castle, to strike at what was considered one of the most powerful outposts of the city of Florence. Reconquered by the city of the lily, it was besieged by the Sienese and, damaged by a fire, was then restored.

Its present appearance is mainly determined by the alterations carried out around 1860 at the command of Bettino Ricasoli.

Of the ancient structure what remain are the glacis, the central nucleus, part of the bastions and the vaults and, especially, the interesting Chapel of San Jacopo.

Villa Cerna.

The Chapel was built in 1348. It is mostly decorated with mosaics and preserves the tombs of several of the members of the Ricasoli family.

In the Palazzo del Signore - a building of large proportions and in Gothic style - the dining room is especially worthy of admiration, where precious hangings of Flemish workmanship and a collection of period armour are housed.

The rooms which are quite rightly most famous are, however, the **Cellars**: here are kept the wines with the Brolio denomination, the pride of Italian wine production. Along the road which leads from Siena to Florence lie villages and farms immersed in the green of the vineyards.

Worthy of mention is **Lilliano**, of mediaeval origin as is its Parish Church of Santa Cristina; **Villa Cerna**, a building standing on the ruins of the Church of Saints Donato and Cesareo and above all the atmospheric town of Monteriggioni.

MONTERIGGIONI

A picturesque and attractive village on the left bank of the Staggia stream in the Val d'Elsa. It was built in the 13th century for the people of Siena as a castle and advanced outpost of the city. Later it was surrounded with a massive circle of walls with 14 large towers, which in the past were much higher («Sulla cerchia tonda / Monteriggion di torri si corona», as Dante says in the Inferno), to this day, these towers give the place a very picturesque aspect.

Monteriggioni.

USEFUL TOURIST INFORMATION

Emergency telephone numbers:

EMERGENCIES Tel.113
Red Cross (Misericordia)
. . . . .Tel.222199
Medical Service:
Nights and Sundays . . .Tel.586466
Public Assistance Tel.280110
Hospital Tel.585807
Police Tel.201111
Carabinieri Tel.112
Traffic Police Tel.47047
ACI - Breakdown recovery service
Tel.116
Fire Brigade Tel.115
Town Hall Tel.292230
Traffic Wardens Tel.292550
Telephone S.I.P.
Via Termini (8am-9pm) .Tel.43311

A.P.T. (Tourist Information)

Via di Città, 43 . . . . .Tel.42209
Tourist Service Centre
Via Il Campo, 56 . . . . . .Tel.280551
Travel Office SFTI
Exchange Service Tel.283004
Camping Siena Colleverde
Strada Scacciapensieri 37
From 1/4 to 15/10 Swimming pool
Tel.280044

Taxis:

Piazza Matteotti Tel.289350
Piazza Rosselli Tel.44504
Radio Taxi Tel.49222

MUSEUMS - GALLERIES - CHURCHES (opening times)

Town Hall - Piazza del Campo:
Exhibition Rooms and Town Museum. Torre del Mangia: 1st October - 31st March: 8.30am-1.30pm. From 1st April - 30th September: 9.30am-7.30pm. Free Entrance.

National Picture Gallery - Palazzo Buonsignori:
Via S. Pietro 29 - 8.45am-1.45pm - Sundays 9am-1pm - Mondays closed -Free Entrance.

Opera Metropolitana - Museum - Piazza del Duomo:
November-February: 9.30am-2pm - Sundays 9.30am-1pm - 3pm-6pm - March-April - May-October: 9am-1pm - 3pm-6pm - Sundays 9am-1pm - 3pm-5pm June July August September: 9am-1pm - 3pm-7pm - Sundays 9am-1pm. Free Entrance. Reduction for parties of more than ten.

Piccolomini Library - In the Cathedral:
open from 9am until the Cathedral closes. Free Entrance.

Municipal Archive - Piccolomini Palace:
Banchi di Sotto 52. Weekdays 9am-1pm, Saturdays from 9am-12. Sundays closed. Free Entrance.

Etruscan Archaeological Museum:
Piazza del Duomo
Weekdays: 9am-2pm - Holidays and Sundays 9am-1pm. Free Entrance. Closed on Wednesdays.

Municipal Library of the Intronati:
Via della Sapienza 5. Weekdays from 9am-8pm. Sundays and holidays closed. From the 1st to 15th July closed. Free Entrance.

Sanctuary and House of Saint Catherine:
Costa di S. Antonio. Open every day from 7am-12 and 3.30pm-6pm. Free entrance (donations welcome).

Oratory of San Bernardino:
Piazza S. Francesco. Apply to the custodian to visit.

EVENTS:

MAY 3-4: National Celebrations in honour of Saint Catherine of Siena -Patron Saint of Italy.

MAY 25: Drawing of lots at the Town Hall for the three Districts to take part, together with the seven entitled to compete, in the Palio on the 2nd July.

JUNE 29: In the morning, selection trials of the horses presented to the Municipality and later "assignment by lot" of the ten horses of the Districts to compete in the Palio on the 2nd July. At 7pm the Districts will make the first trial run in the Piazza del Campo.

JUNE 30: The trial runs of the Districts continue in preparation for the Palio: they take place: at 9am and 7pm.

JULY 1: At 9am the fourth trial run takes place, and in the evening the dress rehearsal is held. Late in the evening the "propitiatory dinner" is held, attended by all the "contradaioli", their agents and the rider who will race in the Palio. Tourists wishing to follow closely these interesting popular events may also attend this dinner.

JULY 2 - THE PALIO

In the morning the final test takes place in the Piazza del Campo. Early in the afternoon, there is the blessing of the horses and riders who are to take part in the dangerous tournament. At 6pm the Historical Procession, greeted by the solemn notes of the bell from the Campanile of the Torre del Mangia, enters the Piazza del Campo, and at 7pm the race is run.

JULY 13: Drawing of lots at the Town Hall for the three Districts to take part, together with the seven entitled to compete, in the Palio of August 16th.

AUGUST 13: In the morning, selection trials of the horses and subsequent "assignment by lot" to the Districts taking part in the Palio on August 16th. In the afternoon the first trial run in Piazza del Campo.

AUGUST 14: The trial runs continue at 9am and at 6.30pm.

AUGUST 14: Historical Procession of the Votive Candle offered to the Blessed Virgin of the Assumption, the Patron Saint of Siena and of its ancient State, in the presence of the Authorities and of the Pages of the 17 Districts.

AUGUST 15: Ceremonies in the Cathedral in honour of the Blessed Virgin of the Assumption, Patron Saint of Siena, in honour of whom the Palio will be run.

Official award of the gold "Mangia" and the silver "Mangia", the symbolic decorations conferred upon those who have distinguished themselves for cultural, scientific, industrial and commercial activities for the benefit of the City of Siena. The fourth trial run takes place at 9am and the dress rehearsal at 6.30pm.

AUGUST 16 - THE PALIO

At 9am the final test takes place, and in the afternoon the blessing of the horses and riders who will run in the Palio. At 5.30pm the Historical Procession makes its triumphal entry into the Piazza del Campo: symbolically, the glory of the ancient Republic of Siena comes to life again. At 6.30pm the race is run.

DECEMBER 13 - Celebrations in honour of Santa Lucia, with a market of pottery, terracotta and majolica-ware which is held in the adjacent streets. The dates of other events - or conferences of an artistic and cultural nature - are published in the Tourist Calendar Booklet, issued annually by the Official Tourist Office of Siena.

EXHIBITIONS AND MARKETS

Permanent Display of Italian Wines:

Fortezza Medicea - Tel.42497. This is the most important activity of the "Autonomous Authority for the Display and Sale of Characteristic and Vintage Wines". Opened in 1960 it was set up with the help of the Ministries of Trade and Industry, Agriculture and Forestry, and Tourism, as well as with that of the **Monte dei Paschi di Siena** and of the local **Chamber of Commerce**. Housed in the 16th century Fortezza Medicea, the "Enoteca Italica" uses its underground premises for the permanent display of Italian vintage wines which have been previously checked and selected by a special official Commission of Experts as a guarantee to consumers; there are also basement rooms for relaxation and wine-tasting in a suitably furnished, picturesque and welcoming setting.

A restaurant with menus suited to each wine is available after the tasting.

SIENA: HOTELS - PENSIONS - RESTAURANTS

Hotel:Cat. Class-Kat.

***** PARK HOTEL
Via Marciano, 16 . . . . .Tel. 44803
**** ATHENA
Via P. Mascagni, 55 . . . . . . .Tel. 286313
****JOLLY EXCELSIOR
P.zza La Lizza, 1 . . . . .Tel. 288448
****LA CERTOSA
Via di Certosa, 82 . . . . .Tel. 288180
****VILLA PATRIZIA
Via Fiorentina, 58 . . . . .Tel. 50431
****VILLA SCACCIAPENSIERI
Via di Scacciapensieri,10
. . . . .Tel. 41441
***CASTAGNETO
Via dei Cappuccini, 39 . . . . .Tel. 45103
***CONTINENTALE
Via Banchi di Sopra, 85
. . . . .Tel. 41451
***DUOMO
Via Stalloreggi,38 . . . . .Tel. 289088
***GARDEN
Via Custoza,2 . . . . .Tel. 47056
***ITALIA
Viale Cavour, 67 . . . . .Tel. 41177
***LA TOSCANA
Via Cecco Angiolieri, 12
. . . . .Tel. 46097
***MINERVA
Via Garibaldi, 72 . . . . .Tel. 284474
***MODERNO
Via B. Peruzzi, 19 . . . . . . .Tel. 288019
***PALAZZO RAVIZZA
Pian dei Mantellini, 34
. . . . .Tel. 280462
***SANTA CATERINA
Via E.S. Piccolomini, 7
. . . . .Tel. 221105
***VICO ALTO
Via delle Regioni, 26 . . . . . .Tel. 48571
**ALEX
Via G.Gigli,5 . . . . .Tel. 220338
**CANNON D'ORO
Via Montanini, 28 . . . . .Tel. 44321
**CENTRALE
Via Calzoleria, 24 . . . . .Tel. 280379
**CHIUSARELLI
Via Curtatone, 9 . . . . .Tel. 280562
**LEA
V.le XXIV Maggio, 10 . . . . .Tel. 283207
**PICCOLO HOTEL IL PALIO
P.zza del Sale, 19 . . . . .Tel. 281131

RESTAURANTS
(closing day)

AL MARSILI
Via del Castoro, 3 . .Tel. 47154 (Mon.)
ANTICA BOTTEGANOVA
Strada Chiantigiana, 29
. . . . .Tel. 284230
(Sun. and Mon. lunchtime)
GROTTA DI S. CATERINA
Via della Galluzza, 24
. . . . .Tel. 282208 (Mon.)
IL BIONDO
Via del Rustichetto, 10
. . . . .Tel. 280739 (Wed.)
IL GIARDINO (Hotel) Via B. Peruzzi, 43.
. . . . .Tel. 221197 (Wed.)
L'ANGOLO
Via Garibaldi, 15
. . . . .Tel. 289251 (Sat..)
TAVERNA DI CECCO
Via C. Angiolieri, 19
. . . . .Tel. 288518 (Thu.)
LE CAMPANE
Via delle Campane, 4
. . . . .Tel. 284035 (Mon.)
DA MUGOLONE
Via dei Pellegrini, 8
. . . . .Tel. 283235 (Thu.)
OSTERIA DA CICE
Via S. Pietro, 38
. . . . .Tel. 288026 (Sun.)
RENZO
P.zza Indipendenza
Tel. 289296 (Wed. evenings and Thu.)
SOTTOLEFONTI
Via. E. Fontebranda, 100
. . . . .Tel. 286302 (Thu.)
AI TRE CRISTI
Vicolo Provenzano, 1
. . . . .Tel. 280608 (Mon.)
AL MANGIA
P.zza Il Campo, 42
. . . . .T. 281121 (Mon.)
GUIDORICCIO
Via G. Dupré, 2
. . . . .Tel. 44350 (Sun.)
IL CAMPO
P.zza Il Campo, 50
. . . . .Tel. 280725 (Tue.)
IL VERROCCHIO
Logge del Papa, 1
. . . . .Tel. 284062 (Wed.)
GUIDO
Vicolo Pier Pettinaio, 7
. . . . .Tel. 280042 (Mon.)
LE LOGGE
Via del Porrione, 33 . . . . . . .Tel. 48013
LE TRE CAMPANE
Via Monna Agnese, 2
. . . . .Tel. 286091 (Ven.)
MEDIO EVO
Via dei Rossi, 40
. . . . .Tel. 280315 (Thu.)
SEVERI NO
Via del Capitano, 6 . . . . . .Tel. 288094
TURIDDO
Via Diacceto, 3 . . . .Tel. 282121 (Sat..)
ALLA SPERANZA
P.zza Il Campo, 33
. . . . .Tel. 280190 (Wed.)
ZI' ROSA
P.zza Il Campo, 13
. . . . .Tel. 281123 (Thu.)

INDEX

© Copyright
CASA EDITRICE PERSEUS - PLURIGRAF collection
Published and printed by Centro Stampa Editoriale, Sesto Fiorentino, (Fi).

Collective work. All rights reserved.
No part of this publication may be reproduced, or transmitted in any form or by any means,
whether electronic, chemical, or mechanical, photocopying, or otherwise (including cinema,
television, and any information storage and retrieval system) without the express
written permission of the publisher.